Roosters of the Apocalypse

Rael Jean Isaac

Roosters of the Apocalypse

Published by The Heartland Institute
One South Wacker Drive #2740
Chicago, Illinois 60606
phone 312/377-4000
fax 312/377-5000
www.heartland.org

Additional copies of this book
are available from The Heartland Institute
for the following prices:

1-10 copies	$8.95 per copy
11-50 copies	$7.95 per copy
51-100 copies	$6.95 per copy
101 or more	$5.95 per copy

Printed and manufactured in the United States of America
ISBN-13 978-1-934791-37-0
ISBN-10 1-934791-37-7

2 3 4 5 6 7

Contents

Introduction

Beginning in the spring of 1856, the Xhosa tribe in today's South Africa destroyed its own economy. The Xhosa killed an estimated half-million of their own cattle (which they ordinarily treated with great care and respect), ceased planting crops, and destroyed their grain stores. By the end of 1857 between thirty and fifty thousand of them had starved to death—a third to a half of the population. The British herded survivors of the once-powerful tribe into labor camps, and white settlers took much of their land.

The Xhosa had acted on the prophecy of a 15-year-old girl who promised that if they destroyed all they had and purified themselves of "witchcraft" (including evil inclinations and selfishness), the world before the white invaders came would be restored: The British oppressors would flee, and the Xhosa ancestors would return, bringing with them an even greater abundance of cattle and grain.[1]

Do you feel a mixture of pity and contempt for these strange people who ruined themselves on the basis of an outlandish vision? If so, the feeling is misplaced. Just as the basis for the Xhosa economy was cattle, the lifeblood of our economy is energy. And we are strangling our own energy supply on the basis of an apocalyptic prophecy that has no more validity than the one that sent the Xhosa spinning into cultural self-immolation.

The apocalyptic vision to which we subscribe has a superficial scientific gloss—"climate change"—making it palatable to the modern mind, but at bottom both visions prescribe economic suicide. And both promise self-sacrifice will bring about a golden age. In the case of the Xhosa, that golden age was the time before the British invaded. In our own, to quote famed environmentalist David Brower (director of the Sierra Club and then of Friends of the Earth), it's "back there about a century when, at the start of the Industrial Revolution we began applying energy in vast amounts to tools with which we began tearing the environment apart."[2]

Chapter 1
Roosters vs. Owls

Apocalyptic movements have much in common with one another, no matter the gulf in time and educational level of the participants. In *Heaven on Earth: The Varieties of the Millennial Experience*, Boston University historian Richard Landes describes the appeal of these movements, their chief characteristics, how they take over societies (and eventually run out of steam), and their impact.

Landes describes those who initiate and build support for these movements as roosters, for they crow an exciting new message, and their opponents as owls, gloomsters counseling caution and skepticism. Roosters will drown out the warning owls only if they rally elites to their cause, and elites are a hard sell—especially, says Landes, in the case of prophecies demanding a society self-mutilate. That means enthusiasm must first be generated in a sufficient segment of the public to put pressure on elites to go along.

Once the authorities pronounce themselves in favor of the prophecy and it "pays" to believe, many more ordinary people will join in.[3] In the case of the Xhosa, the initial rooster was a simple orphan girl. The key to the triumph of her vision was her uncle, a well-known preacher and diviner who preached her message and convinced the chiefs – including the chief of chiefs, named Sarhili – of its truth.[4]

Later we will describe the origin of the climate change prophecy. Here let us note the astonishing speed of its dissemination and the number and political power of its converts. If Landes is right that elites are normally a hard sell when it comes to self-destructive enthusiasms, in this case they have been won over with breathtaking ease. For example, here's U.S. Senate Majority Leader Harry Reid: "Coal makes us sick. Oil makes us sick. It's global warming. It's ruining our country. It's ruining our world."[5] At a World Economic Forum on climate in Davos in February 2009, Vaclav Klaus, former president of Czechoslovakia, found himself a solitary owl in a sea of leading politicians and heads of state. "I looked around in vain to find at least one person who would share my views—there was no one. All the participants at the meeting took man-made global warming for granted."[6]

The governing boards of many scientific associations in the United States endorse the movement.[7] Elite international scientific associations, including the U.K.'s venerable Royal Society, are also on board. Then there's the media, which eagerly provide a platform and echo chamber for the most terrifying apocalyptic scenarios the roosters can conjure up: seas rising twenty feet to drown Manhattan, the Netherlands, and Bangladesh; a shutdown in "thermohaline convection" in the oceans plunging Europe into a new ice age; multiplying hurricanes and tornadoes; an end to polar bears; a vast increase in malaria, dengue fever, Ebola virus, and a cornucopia of other diseases. That's just a partial list of what a single noisy rooster – Al Gore – promises man-made global warming will bring upon us.[8] Sir Nicholas Stern, the London School of Economics professor then-Prime Minister Tony Blair chose to lead a team of economists to study climate change, has prophesied "extended world war" and the need to move "hundreds of millions, probably billions of people."[9]

As the apocalypse bandwagon gets rolling, it gathers momentum. More and more people develop a stake in it. Scientists depend on government grants, and grants go to projects proposed by climate roosters, not owls. Between 1993 and 2010, according to the Government Accountability Office, the federal government poured almost $107 billion into such projects.[10]

Giant corporations see dollar signs in government-subsidized solar and wind power and in trading carbon credits under cap-and-trade schemes. They become deep-pocket lobbyists for the apocalypse. The U.S. Climate Action Partnership includes such stalwarts of capitalism as GE, Caterpillar, DuPont, General Motors, PepsiCo, ConocoPhillips, and Ford, all egging on Washington "to quickly enact strong national legislation to require significant reductions of greenhouse gas emissions."[11]

(ConocoPhillips and Caterpillar subsequently have announced plans to drop out of the partnership.[12])

There are now more than four climate change lobbyists for each member of Congress.[13] Then there are the "consultants" on climate change and the lawyers salivating at the prospect of billions of dollars in damages from laggard "emitters." There is even a new breed of "eco-therapists" to help people navigate their feelings of fear, grief, confusion, and depression about contributing to global warming.[14]

Active apocalyptic movements are urgent. It's now or never. If action is not taken quickly, it will be too late. Xhosa believers set about destroying their cattle and grain immediately. United Nations Secretary General Ban Ki-moon (the global warming apocalypse owes more to the U.N. than to any other single institution) told the Global Environmental Forum in 2009, "We have just four months. Four months to secure the future of our planet."[15] More generously, Prince Charles in March 2009 gave us "100 months to alter our behavior before we risk catastrophic climate change and the unimaginable horror that this would bring."[16]

Fostering the sense of urgency, roosters advance the notion of "a tipping point" after which the worst is upon us, no matter what we do. James Hansen, director of NASA's Goddard Institute for Space Studies (perhaps the most vociferous of the scientifically credentialed roosters) warns of irreversible effects if we don't act quickly: "As species are exterminated by shifting climate zones, ecosystems can collapse. ... The greatest danger hanging over our children and grandchildren is initiation of changes that will be irreversible on any time scale that humans can imagine."[17] The most far-out speculation of all comes from researchers at Pennsylvania State University, who suggest rising greenhouse emissions could tip off aliens that we are a rapidly growing threat to the universe – and lead them to take drastic action against Earth before the threat escalates further.[18]

Given the sweeping success of the climate change movement, you might think its roosters would disregard the vastly outnumbered owls, leaving them to naysay, ignored, on the margins. But that's not how apocalyptic movements work. Unanimity is terribly important. As in the story of the emperor's new clothes, one small voice at the right moment can expose the nakedness of the project. So dissenters must be silenced, discredited – or worse.

As the ancestors failed to appear and the Xhosa believers began to starve, they blamed the stubborn owls who had kept their cattle. Arguing it was their disbelief that delayed the return of the ancestors, the believers began to kill the cattle of those they called the amagogotya, the selfish hard ones, those who "eat alone."[19] In the global warming apocalypse, every effort is made to banish climate change owls, no matter how distinguished their scientific record, to the outer fringe. The owls are flat-earthers, patsies for big oil, "deniers" (as in Holocaust deniers), analogous to racists (Al Gore's contribution),[20] "people who say that asbestos is as good as talcum powder" (this from Rajendra Pachauri, chairman of the U.N.'s Intergovernmental Panel on Climate Change).[21] James Hansen says CEOs of fossil energy companies should be tried for "high crimes against humanity and nature."[22]

Manufacturing Consensus

This passion for total agreement accounts for the "Climategate" scandal that enveloped researchers at the Climatic Research Unit at the University of East Anglia, who serve as gatekeepers for the Intergovernmental Panel on Climate Change (IPCC). In November 2009 a hacker downloaded candid e-mails among top climate roosters in England, the United States, and elsewhere between 1996 and 2009. The messages bemoan recalcitrant data that fail to support the claim of "unprecedented warming," describe the tricks (their term) used to coax the data to buttress the theory, report efforts to keep the views of scientific dissenters out of reputable journals and U.N. reports, and boast of deletion of data to make it unavailable to other researchers.[23]

The e-mailers sound much more like hardcore zealots than scrupulous seekers of scientific fact. For example, Phil Jones, director of the Climatic Research

Unit, e-mailed major rooster Michael Mann regarding a couple of skeptical articles: "I can't see either of these papers being in the next IPCC report. Kevin [Trenberth] and I will keep them out somehow, even if we have to redefine what the peer-review literature is!"[24]

While Climategate has received the most attention, the way the series of IPCC reports – which provide the scientific underpinning for the entire climate change movement – are edited is rife with scandal. In *Climate of Corruption*, Larry Bell describes what happened to the crucial Chapter 8 in the IPCC's 1995 *Second Assessment Report*. The final draft stated there was insufficient evidence to connect observed climate changes to man-made greenhouse gases. Here are a few of the conclusions, which were based on reviews of 130 peer-reviewed scientific studies: "None of the studies cited above has shown clear evidence that we can attribute the observed [climate] changes to the specific cause of increases in greenhouse gases." "Any claims of positive detection and attribution of significant climate change are likely to remain controversial until uncertainties in the total natural variability of the climate system are reduced." "When will an anthropogenic effect on climate be identified? It is not surprising that the best answer to this question is, 'We do not know.'"[25]

Bell tells us what happened on the way to publication:

That chapter, which should have governed the entire IPCC report, was then substantially rewritten to advance a global warming campaign being waged by the UN, the NGOs, and the White House [Gore was vice-president]. In May 1996, after the report was released, the Chapter 8 conclusions were startlingly different from the scientists' accepted version. The Chapter 8 lead author, Ben Santer, from the U.S. government's Lawrence Livermore National Laboratory, had excised denials of any scientific evidence of manmade global warming, replacing them with statements asserting just the opposite: "The body of statistical evidence in Chapter 8, when examined in the context of our physical understanding of the climate system, now points to a discernible human influence on the global climate". ... The "discernible human influence" insertion, which reversed the entire IPCC climate science report, purportedly ended all debate on this matter, providing an official foundation for the UN-sponsored Kyoto Protocol to follow in 1997.[26]

Thus, according to Bell, a misrepresentation provided the basis for a huge international commitment to transform energy use. Moreover, the roosters did their dirty work unscathed. Frederick Seitz, former president of the National Academy of Sciences and former president of Rockefeller University, wrote an op-ed in *The Wall Street Journal* in which he noted, "I have never witnessed a more disturbing corruption of the peer-review process than the events that led to this IPCC report."[27] *The Wall Street Journal* wrote an editorial critical of the IPCC, and the journal *Nature*, although favoring adoption of the Kyoto Protocol, had the decency to disapprove of the IPCC's rewriting of Chapter 8.[28] But that was all, and the apocalypse rolled on.

The writers of the hacked e-mails, Santer among them,[29] comprise most of the core scientific roosters who keep the apocalypse going. They serve as lead authors, contributing authors, and editors shaping the contents of the series of IPCC reports. Although much of the respect accorded the reports is due to their literal weight (they are each upwards of 800 pages), their impact comes from the brief *Summaries for Policymakers*, which are all the reporters – who disseminate the reports' findings – read. These summaries are formulated by the hardcore roosters and then gone over line by line, revised and agreed to, by representatives of member governments. Of course, this process has zero resemblance to the way real scientific research is reviewed and published.[30] But the summaries accomplish their purpose in keeping up the heat, each report claiming the apocalypse is approaching even sooner than the last one predicted.

In between reports, the roosters hold a steady stream of conferences and congresses to ramp up the pressure for dramatic action now. For example, in March 2009 the University of Copenhagen hosted a congress on climate change attended by 2,000 scientists from more than seventy countries. A 36-page summary "for laymen" of its findings was presented to a meeting of European Union leaders in Brussels assembled to discuss climate change. That summary warned of escalating "tipping points," proclaimed the Great Barrier Reef was in danger, and cautioned, "To recover ecosystems like that would likely take hundreds of thousands, if not many millions of years. ... We cannot afford to take a business as usual approach. ... Future generations will inherit an unlivable planet."[31]

Even all this understates the transgressions of the IPCC. In *The Delinquent Teenager Who Was Mistaken for the World's Top Climate Expert*, journalist Donna Laframboise has exposed the full range of deceptive techniques and fakery practiced by the IPCC. While the title may suggest a flippant or superficial take on the issues, Laframboise has performed an astonishing feat of investigative journalism, all the more impressive given that she had retired from her journalistic career and was working as a solitary blogger, with none of the resources of the literally thousands of journalists worldwide who have covered the IPCC with mindless, slavish devotion.[32]

Chapter 2
Apocalyptic Jazz

Landes notes apocalypses adapt to changed circumstances – he calls this process apocalyptic jazz. In the case of the Xhosa, as conditions deteriorated and the ancestors failed to show up on successive promised dates, the emphasis shifted from self-blame (we held back a few cattle; we sold some cattle; we did not sufficiently purify ourselves of witchcraft) to blaming the owls: unanimity of belief and action was required for the prophecy to be fulfilled. Things got ugly as roosters began to destroy the cattle of recalcitrant owls.[33]

The process by which "global warming" morphed into "climate change" is a good example of apocalyptic jazz. Starting in 2002, the world unexpectedly stopped warming even as carbon dioxide levels continued their steady rise. To the great chagrin of the roosters, none of the twenty multimillion-dollar supercomputers on which they based their predictions had foreseen this.[34] Substituting "climate change" for "global warming" solved the problem.

Asked about the global warming pause, U.S. Senator Debbie Stabenow (D-Mich.) produced this conversation-stopper: "But climate change is not just about temperatures going up. It's also about volatility."[35] Whatever the climate's gyrations, man's "carbon footprint" is responsible. Tsunamis, cyclones, earthquakes, hurricanes, tornadoes, floods, famines, droughts, heat waves, cold waves, decades of ascending or descending temperatures – all can be deposited at the door of human-caused climate change.

But if this piece of apocalyptic jazz has the advantage of being impervious to disproof, it has a fundamental (if generally unremarked) problem. Global warming rests on a scientific theory buttressed by two undisputed facts. The facts: (1) Burning fossil fuels increases the concentration of carbon dioxide in the atmosphere, which is estimated to have risen about 38 percent during the Industrial Age. (2) Temperatures have risen approximately 1.3 degrees Fahrenheit over the past century.

The theory: The higher concentration of carbon dioxide raises the Earth's temperature, leading to increased humidity and water vapor (a greenhouse gas) causing a further increase in Earth's temperature (so-called positive feedback). It is on the basis of such feedback that larger increases in temperature are projected into the future if carbon dioxide emissions are not cut back.

But what is the scientific theory underpinning *climate change*? The climate has shifted dramatically over time, clearly without benefit of human activity. Twenty thousand years ago, a mere moment in geologic time, what is now Chicago was buried under ice a mile thick. Climate change is not a scientific theory; it is a banal statement of the obvious.

Reframing the Issue

Another way global warming campaigners have adapted to changed circumstances is to reframe the issue and then claim the critics' objections have been answered. In the wake of Climategate, owls were emboldened. To deal with this problem, University of California physics professor Richard A. Muller wrote an op-ed in the European *Wall Street Journal* on October 21, 2011, in which he disseminated prior to peer review (an unusual act in itself) the results of a two-year study conducted under his leadership, the Berkeley Earth Surface Temperature Project (BEST). The haste to report these findings is especially odd because they are thoroughly uncontroversial: The Earth has been warming since 1950.

As we have noted, the rise in temperatures over the past century is one of the undisputed facts on which global warming theory is based. It's true there has been controversy over the siting of some of the stations at which temperatures are measured, especially in urban areas where cement and surrounding buildings can raise temperatures artificially. The conclusion of the BEST study is that although the concerns are justified – "the temperature-station quality is largely awful," says

Muller – even when low-quality stations are eliminated, the results hold, the Earth has warmed.[36]

However, Muller's op-ed made it seem the BEST study did more than confirm something on which there is general agreement. He begins his essay, "Are you a global warming skeptic?" and declares that after his study "you should not be a skeptic, at least not any longer." But a global warming skeptic is not someone who doubts the world has warmed; it is someone who is skeptical that the warming is primarily man-made. Muller makes it seem as if global warming necessarily implies human causation, thus neatly burying the debate. Only at the conclusion does he cover himself by saying, "How much of the warming is due to humans and what will be the likely effects? We made no independent assessment of that."[37] In other words, if you make your way to the very end, you discover the BEST studies are irrelevant to the fundamental dispute.

But if the BEST studies are irrelevant to the scientific debate, Muller has ensured they are not irrelevant to *public perception* of that debate. *The Washington Post* published an article headlined, "A Skeptical Physicist Ends Up Confirming Climate Data"[38] (what is more convincing than a supposedly skeptical scientist being won over by the data?).To the average reader, who probably doesn't go much beyond the headline, this sounds like vindication of the beleaguered climate roosters.

The U.K.'s *The Guardian* picked up the story under the equally misleading headline, "Global Warming Study Finds No Grounds for Climate Skeptics." The article included an interview with Muller in which he declared, "My hope is that this will win over those people who are properly skeptical. Some people lump the properly skeptical in with the deniers and that makes it easy to dismiss them, because the deniers pay no attention to science."[39] But who are the "deniers" in climate change parlance, if not those who question that global warming is man-made? Muller attempts to shut down the real climate debate by arguing the BEST study has ended the legitimate aspect (putting to rest the concerns of those who worried about the readings at climate stations), with remaining critics being illegitimate "deniers" who pay no attention to science.

Post-Normal Science

One of the most astonishing examples of apocalyptic jazz comes from Mike Hulme, professor of climate change [sic] at the University of East Anglia and a key player in shaping the IPCC reports. In his book *Why We Disagree About Climate Change*,[40] Hulme does not make the familiar claim that "the science is settled." On the contrary, he admits "uncertainty pervades scientific predictions about the future performance of global and regional climates. And uncertainties multiply when considering all the consequences that might follow from such changes in climate." But for Hulme this does not suggest we "first, do no harm" and go slow in transforming our economies. Instead, it suggests we toss science, as traditionally understood,[41] out the window. Hulme asserts, "climate change has become a classic example of what philosophers of science Silvio Funtowicz and Jerry Ravetz have termed 'post-normal science': the application of science to public issues where 'facts are uncertain, values in dispute, stakes high and decisions urgent.'"[42]

In "post-normal science," consensus substitutes for science, with government bureaucracies discerning and then acting on the recommendations of scientists they select.[43] Thanks to the jazz of post-normal science, global warming morphs from a scientific theory (capable of being disproved) into "an intellectual resource around which our collective and personal identities and projects can form and take shape."[44] According to Hulme, because the idea of climate change is "so plastic," it "can serve many of our psychological, ethical, and spiritual needs." Thus, as Hulme sees it, "We need to ask not what we can do for climate change, but to ask what climate change can do for us."[45]

A self-avowed socialist, Hulme clearly sees climate change as a useful tool for promoting population control, income redistribution, and "sustainable development," i.e. putting the brakes on development. Others are presumably free to use climate change to advance different projects. But if we have transcended science for "post-normal science" and climate change, drenched in values, is whatever we choose to make of it, disinterested scientific debate on the truth or falsity of man-made global warming is beside the point.

The Owl's Perspective

Landes writes that past apocalyptic prophecies have, without exception, been wrong. Of course, there's always a first time. But given that 100 percent failure record, surely the owls deserve a hearing. The owls contend natural cycles shaped by sun and sea play a far more important role than greenhouse gases in determining global temperature. They point out that over past glacial and interglacial periods, rising temperatures *preceded* rising carbon dioxide levels, as warming oceans released carbon dioxide. They say variation in the sun's energy output correlates better with the Earth's temperature over time than do carbon dioxide levels.[46]

The owls emphasize that the catastrophic predictions advanced by global warming theorists rely not on empirical data but on untested computer models. Despite the faith roosters put in them – Bill McKibben, one of the most energetic popularizers of the coming Armageddon, tells us of "a sophisticated [climate] software model that could instantly analyze any proposal and tell you what it would mean a hundred years down the road"[47] – models are no better than the data they are fed. The models, for example, pay no attention to the effect of cosmic rays on clouds. A groundbreaking experiment at the CERN particle physics laboratory in Geneva reported on in *Nature* in 2011 suggests this may be an important factor.[48] Moreover, theoretical physics professor Freeman Dyson observes current climate models "do a very poor job of describing the clouds, the dust, the chemistry and the biology of fields and farms and forests. They do not begin to describe the real world."[49]

Although the 100-years-out predictions cannot be tested, empirical evidence calls into question the reliability of the models. For example, NASA satellite data for 2000–2011 reveal more energy is lost to space during and after warming than the climate models predict (i.e., heat is not trapped in the atmosphere to the extent assumed by the models).[50] Although the models emphasize positive feedback, satellite observations suggest they ignore the negative feedback produced by clouds and water vapor that diminish the warming effects of carbon dioxide.[51]

The Arctic was supposed to be the canary in the coal mine, the first place on the planet to show man-made global warming. Yet findings published in the *Journal of Glaciology* show a strong rise in temperatures in about 1920, peaking in the 1930s, with no warming in the last eighty years of the twentieth century.[52] And whereas the models predict the Antarctic would warm, in fact Antarctic ice has been growing.[53] The models predict the middle atmosphere will warm faster than the surface, but observations show the opposite.[54]

The owls also point out that the roosters fudge the historical record. If the Earth was warmer in the past than it is now, natural cycles may be more important than human activity in determining temperature. That's where Michael Mann and the famous hockey stick come in.

Climate roosters faced the problem of what to do about the Medieval Warm Period, an era of warm global temperatures from around 950 to 1300 A.D., when Greenland was warm enough for the Vikings to create a flourishing settlement. Climate researcher Dr. David Deming of the University of Oklahoma testified before the U.S. Senate about the reaction he received when he published an article about the Medieval Warm Period in *Science* in 1995: "I received an astonishing e-mail from a major researcher in the area of climate change. He said, 'We have to get rid of the Medieval Warm Period'. ... In 1999 Michael Mann and his colleagues published a reconstruction of past temperature in which the Medieval Warm Period simply vanished. ... This unique estimate became known as the 'hockey stick.'"[55] By the time it was discredited by scientists, the hockey stick had been fixed firmly in the public imagination. The IPCC's *Third Assessment Report* emphasized it; Al Gore featured it in *An Inconvenient Truth*; and the Canadian government mailed a copy of the curve to every household![56]

The attempt to bury the Medieval Warm Period – or failing that, to claim it was localized in England, the Alps, Greenland, and North America[57] – received a body blow with the publication in October 2011 of an analysis by Chinese scientists of tree rings for the past 2,485 years on the central-eastern Tibetan Plateau. The study found the Medieval Warm Period, Little Ice Age, and twentieth century warming all appeared there at the same time they did in other places worldwide. Furthermore, they found the largest amplitude and rate of temperature change occurred during the Eastern Jin Event (343–425 A.D.), not in the late twentieth century. What's more, they found the temperature cycles were associated with solar activity, with cold intervals corresponding to sunspot minimums. Based on these findings, they predicted temperatures will decrease until 2068 A.D. and then increase once more.[58]

Is Global Warming Benign?

The overwhelming focus of attention is on whether global warming is man-made. But from the standpoint of public policy, there is another, even more important question: Is global warming good or bad?

The owls insist the moderate warming we are experiencing is benign. Increased carbon dioxide in the atmosphere means increased rates of plant growth and the ability of plants to grow under drier conditions. Animal life, which depends upon plant life for food, increases proportionately. So does species diversity, which is closely associated with the quantity of plant life per acre.[59]

Warmer weather is also good for human health – there's a reason people move south on retirement. Weather Channel founder John Coleman sums up the owl's perspective: "Our luck to be living in an interglacial period when the Earth is warm and life thrives is the ultimate in good fortune. If we must worry about the future, it seems concern about the onset of nature's next ice age would be a better concern than any about uncontrolled heat."[60]

There are even some roosters, such as Björn Lomborg, author of *The Skeptical Environmentalist*, who are critical of fellow roosters. Lomborg argues that far from posing cataclysmic dangers, warmer temperatures could save 1.4 million lives a year.[61] Besides, he says, there are far more pressing problems – among them hunger, lack of education, child mortality, and diseases such as malaria and AIDS – especially in poor countries, that could be alleviated with a fraction of the funds devoted to climate change.[62] When it comes to climate change, hybrid rooster-owls like Lomborg in effect say, don't pretend to have the power to roll back the waves.

Ways to adapt keep rolling in. For example, a report in the September 2011 *Annals of Botany* says modifying crops to grow longer roots would allow plants naturally to sequester carbon dioxide in the soil – an added bonus is that such plants are more tolerant of drought, flooding, and other challenges.[63]

Chapter 3
Fighting Global Warming with Tax Dollars

Given the host of uncertainties, even a subprime broker at the height of the bubble would be reluctant to underwrite projects to roll back global warming. But apocalyptic movements follow their own rhythms. Henri Desroche compares them to forest fires igniting, spreading, sometimes consuming whole regions, nations, and cultures before passing from the scene.[64]

Landes likens the life-cycle of apocalyptic movements to a series of four waves. First comes the "waxing wave," as roosters, full of passionate conviction, break into public awareness, gaining mass and speed. Second comes the "breaking wave," when roosters, at the peak of their power, dominate public life. This is followed by the "churning wave," when the impetus of the movement carries it past the failure of expectations, members of the group have lost part of their credibility, and the movement must mutate to survive as it goes over the shoreline. Finally comes the receding wave, when owls regain the ascendancy.[65]

From the political point of view, climate change must still be counted a breaking wave. It continues to dominate public life because the preponderance of political, academic, environmental, and media elites, as well as a significant segment of business leaders, remain committed roosters.

Intellectually it's another story. As a result of Climategate the IPCC has lost credibility. The voices and arguments of the owls are finally getting a broader hearing thanks to new scientific studies and the already-obvious failure of global warming forecasting computer models. Intellectually, then, we are in the churning wave stage and some might argue the receding wave is already in plain sight.

Yet because the intellectual shift has not reached political and other decision-shaping elites, Xhosa-like, we remain on track for economic destruction. The Obama administration has set a goal of reducing greenhouse gas emissions by 83 percent below 2005 levels in 2050. Columnist George Will notes acerbically that reducing emissions by 83 percent would mean per-capita emissions would be about what they were in 1875.[66] The only way to accomplish that goal is to sharply cut back on our chief sources of energy: oil, natural gas, and coal. We obtain close to 85 percent of our energy from these major greenhouse gas culprits.

Unlike the Xhosa, our economy won't die in a year. Our politicians and regulators, urged on by the environmental lobby, seek to gradually drive up the costs of oil, coal, and gas to the point that we use much less of them. The complicated arrangements of cap and trade amount to a huge tax on energy. It's hard to improve on Larry Bell's description of how this works:

> [Cap and trade] enables fossil fuel-dependent corporations to promote themselves as being 'carbon neutral' by purchasing 'carbon offsets' from other entities in the form of emissions reductions elsewhere, or by claiming that they are achieving carbon dioxide absorption by planting trees to offset their 'carbon footprints.' You might liken the concept to the sale of indulgences by medieval churches through divine authority. A more contemporary illustration would be to imagine that someone in prison offers to pay for some of your 'good behavior' credits, literally as a 'get-out-of-jail ticket.' The central question would be, how much to you think it would really reduce crime?[67]

Unlike cotton or gold or coffee or oil, carbon credits are a fictitious commodity with an intrinsic value of zero. It is only government legislation rationing emissions that gives them worth. Despite this, Richard Sandor, who headed the now-defunct Chicago Climate Exchange (which once hoped to be the New York Stock Exchange for carbon emission trading) predicted in a January 2009 interview with the *Financial Times* carbon dioxide would become the largest commodity traded in the world market.[68] One thing is sure: Emissions trading is likely to be the biggest source of fraud. Europol, the European criminal intelligence agency, has estimated as much as 90 percent of Europe's carbon trades involves fraudulent activity. According to Oscar Reyes of the watchdog Carbon Trade Watch, "carbon markets are highly susceptible to fraud, given their complexity and the fact that it's not always clear what is being traded."[69]

Some favored (but shortsighted) companies are bribed into supporting cap and trade when governments give them initial "free" allowances to emit carbon dioxide, which they can then "trade" (i.e., sell) to other companies that need energy to function. Cleverly, the carbon tax is disguised from the public, because it is levied not on individuals but on utilities, refiners, gas producers, manufacturers – who, of course, pass the tax on to consumers.

The Heritage Foundation's Center for Data Analysis toted up the costs of the cap and trade bill (deceptively titled the American Clean Energy and Security Act and more familiarly known as Waxman-Markey) that passed the House in June 2009 but didn't make it through the Senate. By 2035, the last year analyzed, annual GDP losses, adjusted for inflation, were $6,790 per family – this before each family paid its $4,600 share of carbon taxes.[70]

As opponents successfully dubbed cap and trade "cap and tax," proponents have resorted to yet more euphemisms, renaming their legislative proposals the

Climate and Energy Bill, or the Climate Bill, or the American Power Act. Whatever the title and whatever the language of the bills, at bottom they are cap and tax.[71]

Renewables to the Rescue?

The roosters say they are not advocating a drastic reduction in our standard of living, for "renewables" will take up the slack. But EPA itself says less than 2 percent of our energy comes from "renewable" sources such as solar, geothermal, biomass, landfill gas, and wind combined. And if you take out ethanol (biomass), which even the U.N. has soured on because it drives up the price of food in poor countries, the share of our energy needs that is met by the much-touted renewables is minuscule. In 2008, solar produced 0.09 percent and wind 0.5 percent of U.S. energy.[72]

It's true that 15.5 percent of our energy – the 7 percent that comes from hydroelectric and the 8.5 percent from nuclear – is largely greenhouse gas emissions-free. But environmentalists dislike hydroelectric (they want the rivers to run free), so there is no reason to expect a renaissance of dams. And although the share of energy provided by nuclear could be dramatically increased if we built new power plants, we haven't built a single one in almost forty years. And in the aftermath of the tsunami that

wreaked havoc on the Fukushima nuclear power
plants in Japan, we are more likely to witness clamor
to shut down existing plants than support for new
construction. The decibels already have risen in the
ongoing battle to close New York's Indian Point
reactors.[73]

Solar and wind, the renewables most acceptable to
the roosters, require huge subsidies; are more
objectionable than coal, oil, or gas on environmental
grounds; and offer zero prospect of replacing fossil
fuels in any foreseeable future. One reason (among
many) is that the more the public experiences them,
the more it hates them. That goes especially for wind
power.

The backlash against renewables is already strong
in Europe. In Denmark, the fact that its heavily
subsidized wind industry accounts for the public's
paying astronomical electric bills – the highest in
Europe – has not deterred the newly elected Danish
government from proposing to completely phase out
fossil fuels by 2050, a remarkable target given that
fossil fuels in 2010 provided 79 percent of Danish
energy. But the new wind turbines are to be built
chiefly offshore. That's because public opposition to
wind turbines has grown sharply, with the number of
civic groups opposing land-based wind power
projects having grown from 40 to 125 just in the past
year.[74]

The Dutch, whose country is synonymous with
windmills, have had enough. Adding wind power to

meet the European Union's target of 20 percent renewable energy sources by 2020 meant adding another 1,000 450-foot-high turbines at a cost of $6 billion. The Dutch want neither these massive blots on the landscape (a state-of-the-art turbine from Czechoslovakia is taller than the Washington monument) nor to pay their cost, and The Netherlands has become the first country to openly abandon the European Union target.[75]

Nor do wind farms displace fossil fuel plants. Belatedly discovering the obvious – that the wind blows only intermittently – Britain has concluded it will have to construct an additional 17 natural gas-powered plants as backup for its new wind turbines, at a cost of ten billion pounds.[76] For the same reason, Germany's 19,000 wind turbines and Denmark's 5,200 have not enabled either country to replace a single coal-fired plant.

In the United States, although lip service to renewables continues strong, on the ground it is another matter. Environmentalists have gone to great lengths to have certain eagles, hawks, and owls protected as endangered species, only to have wind turbines act as avian cuisinarts. In the Bay Area of California, pressure is building to shut down the Altamont Pass Wind Resource Area, which is in the flight path of protected species. It is estimated to kill up to 4,700 birds annually, including almost 1,200 raptors and upwards of 75 golden eagles.[77] One resident of the area protested: "There's a big, big hypocrisy here. If I shoot an eagle it's a $10,000 fine and/or a vacation of one to five years in a federal pen of my choice."[78]

The hypocrisy was underscored when the U.S. attorney for North Dakota hauled seven oil and natural gas companies into federal court for violating the Migratory Bird Treaty Act of 1918 by (inadvertently) being responsible for the death of 28 migratory birds found near oil waste lagoons. As *The Wall Street Journal* noted, "This prosecution is all the more remarkable because the wind industry each year kills not 28 birds ... but some 440,000, according to estimates by the American Bird Conservancy based on Fish and Wildlife Service data. Guess how many legal actions the Obama administration has brought against wind turbine operators under the Migratory Bird Treaty Act? As far as we can tell it's zero."[79]

Wind farms and solar installations take up a great deal of land. To produce the same amount of electrical energy as California's Diablo Canyon nuclear plant, a solar plant would have to cover an area equal to Madison, Wisconsin. This means wind and solar facilities have to be constructed at substantial distances from the people who use them, requiring many miles of high-voltage power lines, which are not only very expensive[80] but also a litigation magnet for those whose land they cross and a standard target of environmental groups. The U.S. Chamber of Commerce's Project No Project, a Web site reporting on thwarted energy infrastructure projects, reports that of three hundred projects delayed or outright killed over the past few years, 65 were for renewables.[81] In short, renewables are not exempt from BANANA, the acronym for Build-Absolutely-Nothing- Anywhere-Near-Anyone.

A Back Door to Kyoto

There is a widespread misconception that the United States has been hanging back in the battle against global warming. That's because Congress did not ratify the 1997 Kyoto Protocol, in which 38 countries and the European Union undertook to lower greenhouse gas emissions by an average of 5 percent from a 1990 baseline by 2012. (The failure to ratify the protocol was not because owls outnumbered roosters in Congress – far from it – but because U.S. senators understood that adopting it would drive still more U.S. manufacturers to China and India, both exempt under the protocol.) Nor, as we have seen, did Congress subsequently pass cap and trade legislation. But this overlooks the extent to which global warming roosters have implemented their campaign successfully through the back door.

One back door route goes through the states. Thirty-nine states have committed to reducing greenhouse gas emissions. Renewable energy mandates are the most popular method. For example, Connecticut passed legislation requiring electric

utilities to purchase 6 percent of their power from
renewables in 2009, going up to 20 percent in 2020.[82]
In 2009 the New Mexico legislature unanimously
raised its 10 percent mandate by 2015 to 15 percent.[83]
California, predictably, is in the vanguard. The 2006
Global Warming Solutions Act (AB 32) requires
reducing greenhouse gas emissions 30 percent by
2020.[84]

Going one better in this potlatch of taxpayer
funds, Los Angeles Mayor Antonio Villaraigosa
announced the city would increase its use of
renewables to 40 percent by 2020.[85] A California
referendum to repeal AB 32 was defeated in 2010 as,
in the words of writer and technology evangelist
George Gilder, "economic sanity lost out in what may
have been the most important election [in the
country]."[86]

Residents of states with mandates pay much more
for energy, although they are unlikely to be aware of
the role mandates play. That's because their bills do
not break out the cost of conventional and renewable
energy. Sometimes there is a hint when their provider
mentions the privilege the customer enjoys of
purchasing wind or solar energy.

States also have bought into cap and trade. The
Northeast Regional Greenhouse Gas Initiative is
farthest along, holding regular carbon-offset
auctions.[87] Originally comprised of ten states, the
regional partnership is down to nine. New Jersey
dropped out, with Gov. Chris Christie giving a biting

farewell, calling it a "failure" and "nothing more than a tax on electricity, a tax on our residents and on businesses with no discernible effect on our environment."[88]

Across the country the Western Climate Initiative, which includes seven states (California among them) and three Canadian provinces, has scheduled auctions to start in 2012. Not to be outdone, nine Midwestern states and the province of Manitoba have signed a Midwestern Greenhouse Gas Reduction Accord to establish their own cap and trade system.[89] All this is well below the radar of the average citizen writing a check to his local utility.

Declaring Carbon Dioxide a Pollutant

Regulation is another backdoor method to reduce carbon dioxide emissions. EPA's most outrageous recent contribution has been to declare carbon dioxide a pollutant. In *The Energy Advocate*, physics professor Howard Hayden neatly sums up the absurdity: If we remove something from the atmosphere and the biosphere benefits, we have removed a pollutant. If we remove something and the biosphere suffers, that something is not a pollutant. If we removed all carbon dioxide, the biosphere would not only suffer, it would die![90]

EPA's road to this milestone finding was unusual. It initially had refused appeals by environmental activists to identify carbon dioxide as a pollutant under the Clean Air Act and was sued by the state of Massachusetts and a coalition of environmental organizations. The U.S. Supreme Court in 2007 ruled in favor of Massachusetts in a 5–4 decision. The majority of the Justices showed a remarkable similarity to the Xhosa tribal leaders who signed on to the cattle-slaying apocalypse. They took on faith the affidavit of a scientist (submitted by one of the environmental outfits) claiming a "strong consensus" of scientists that sea levels would rise "precipitously."

The court concluded the risk of catastrophic harm to Massachusetts "though remote, is nevertheless real" and could be reduced if EPA regulated carbon dioxide.[91] To his credit, Chief Justice John Roberts, in his owl's dissent, called the harms claimed by Massachusetts "pure conjecture" rendering "requirements of imminence and immediacy [of harm] utterly toothless."[92] The Court did leave EPA with an "out": It could offer a "reasonable explanation for why it cannot or will not do so [regulate greenhouse gases]."[93]

While the owlish Bush administration may have been willing to take up the Supreme Court's challenge, it was replaced in 2009 with the rooster-dominated Obama administration. EPA tried to silence those within the organization who opposed the so-called "endangerment finding." EPA scientist Alan Carlin, a 38-year veteran of the organization, described what happened.

In 2009, he was given five days to assess the U.N. studies on which the global warming edifice rested. (Normally he was given six months to a year to evaluate studies produced outside the agency.) He compiled a 98-page report emphasizing that the U.N. reports offered speculation instead of facts. He stated his view – which he did not see as controversial – that EPA "needs to go through the scientific arguments themselves and not rely on what others outside EPA have said." Carlin was told not to discuss his findings with others because, "The administrator and the administration has decided to move forward ... and your comments do not help the legal or policy case for this decision."[94]

EPA officially decided in December 2009 that carbon dioxide is a pollutant, opening the door for it to issue rules regulating the greenhouse gas emissions of everything from hospitals to lawnmowers. Outraged, Michigan Congressman John Dingell (D), one of the original sponsors of the Clean Air Act, said the ruling "had a potential for shutting down virtually all industry and all economic activity and growth."[95] The Heritage Foundation estimated EPA's carbon dioxide regulations would drive up the cost of energy by 30 percent, cost the economy $7 trillion by 2029, and be responsible for annual job losses exceeding 800,000 for several years.[96]

The estimated benefits from reducing temperature are absurdly disproportionate to the economic pain such regulations inflict. To take the largest-scale initiative thus far, the Kyoto Protocol, even if all countries, including the United States, met the emissions targets, it is estimated the global temperature reduction would be about seven hundredths of a degree Celsius by 2050.[97] That's hardly worth mentioning compared to leading rooster James Hansen's estimate that man-made global warming will result in a rise of 2.8 degrees Celsius over the next century.[98] Were Hansen right, a fully implemented Kyoto Protocol would reduce *the projected increase in temperature* by a mere 2.5 percent.

Chapter 4
"Do We Want to
Live or Die?"

Thus far, building on Richard Landes's terminology for millennial movements, we have talked of global warming as an apocalyptic movement and climate change, for example, as apocalyptic jazz, an improvisation by which the message mutates and adapts to circumstances. But in a broader sense global warming itself is merely a "riff" – a passage focusing excitement and energy – in the apocalyptic movement of which it is an outgrowth, namely the modern environmental movement.

Contrary to popular belief, environmentalism did not develop as a reform movement to combat pollution. As Rael Jean Isaac and Erich Isaac wrote in *The Coercive Utopians* in 1983, it was born in a sudden, apocalyptic panic. Earth Day, April 22, 1970, was the date the panic burst upon the national scene. "We are already 5 years into the biosphere self-destruct era" read a sign in the Berkeley, California office of Ecology Action, one of the two hundred environmental groups that mushroomed in the San Francisco area alone during the panic. "The generations now on earth may be the last" read the cover of *The Dying Generations*, a book of readings published in 1971.

Then, as now, politicians were quick to jump on board. Congress closed down for Earth Day, and New York Mayor John Lindsay told an estimated hundred thousand people packed into Union Square that the environmental issue could be summed up simply: "Do we want to live or die?"[99]

From the beginning, energy, not pollution, was the chief target of environmental roosters. Significantly, the focus of the environmentalists' first campaign was nuclear power, the one major source of power – apart from hydro – that in fact produces no pollution. The advantage of this strategy was that it is much easier to scare people about nuclear energy than about coal or oil, even though both of the latter have resulted in far more accidents and deaths.[100]

A Friends of the Earth "public service announcement" was typical. "Announcer: You're looking at America's worst pollution problem. What's that? You say you can't see anything? Of course you can't. This is radio. But that's okay. You couldn't see it anyway. America's worst pollution problem is the radioactive waste that comes out of nuclear power plants."[101]

The campaign was so successful that disarmament groups wound up trying to convince the public that nuclear bombs were as dangerous as nuclear energy. Chemist George Kistakowsky, chairman of the Council for a Livable World, in a February 1981 interview lamented, "We have problems in trying to redirect the public fear of nuclear plants into fear of nuclear war."[102]

The movement's leading roosters did not hold back in affirming their belief that energy – even if it produced no pollution – was the enemy. Amory Lovins (still going strong) announced, "If you ask me, it'd be little short of disastrous for us to discover a source of clean, cheap, abundant energy because of what we would do with it."[103] Paul Ehrlich, of zero population growth fame, declared, "Giving society cheap, abundant energy would be the equivalent of giving an idiot child a machine gun."[104] Then there was Jeremy Rifkin: "The prospect of cheap fusion energy is the worst thing that could happen to the planet."[105]

A Preindustrial Utopia

The roosters of the environmental movement yearn to reinstate a preindustrial utopia. In the introduction we quoted David Brower, who said the lodestar was a century ago, at the start of the Industrial Revolution, before we began to use massive amounts of energy "tearing the environment apart." He said those words in the 1970s, when global warming was not yet so much as a gleam in a U.N. bureaucrat's eye.

John Shuttlesworth, in a Friends of the Earth manual, wrote, "The only really good technology is no technology at all."[106] Life without technology might be physically hard, but it would be spiritually better. Jeremy Rifkin admitted that in the "conserver society" Americans would live a "frugal or Spartan life style," but this would be accepted lovingly "because it is God's order."[107]

E.F. Schumacher's *Small Is Beautiful* was a guide to the beckoning golden age. It's most famous line: "Man is small, therefore, small is beautiful." All man needs to consume, said Schumacher, he should be able to produce himself from beginning to end or jointly with others in the same locality, preferably from renewable resources. (Prince Charles was a big fan of Schumacher[108], as he would subsequently be of global warming dogma – not that his lifestyle, any more than that of Al Gore, coincided with his moral philosophy.) Amory Lovins saw power plants as an assault on human dignity. What he called the "hard path" of fossil fuels entailed dependence on "an alien, remote and perhaps humiliatingly uncontrollable technology run by a far away, bureaucratized technical elite, who have probably never heard of you."[109]

Under a False Flag

The environmental movement has depended for its success on the huge disconnect between the leading roosters, who set the agenda, and the mass of followers. Far from feeling humiliated by modern technology, the average person doesn't give it a thought when he turns on a light switch.

Most people would shudder at the prospect of life without air conditioning, cars, or small or large appliances, all of which had to be sacrificed, according to Maurice Strong, longtime head of the U.N.'s environmental program, to achieve "sustainable development."[110] They do not fancy washing their laundry by hand on the banks of the Monongahela, no matter how lovely the sound of that river's name. But people could be energized by the specter of disease-causing pollution – the roosters claimed a "growing consensus" that most human cancers were environmentally caused – and the unseen terrors of nuclear radiation. And people could be inspired with the idea of preserving especially beautiful open spaces and endangered plant and animal species.

The solution was to appeal for members and funding on the basis of what the public cared about and then act to forward the roosters' mission. Brochures featured regal polar bears and soaring golden eagles, not the furbish lousewort, a fern on whose behalf a $227 million hydroelectric project in Maine was de-authorized by Congress in 1986[111] and whose very name would have been enough to make most Americans vote for the dam.

Also, the roosters were not always as candid as Maurice Strong and Jeremy Rifkin. Lovins promised an exclusive reliance on renewable energy would provide "jobs for the unemployed, capital for business people ... environmental protection for conservationists, better national security for the military, exciting technologies for the secular, a rebirth of religious values for the religious, world order and equity for the globalists, energy independence for isolationists, radical reforms for the young ... civil rights for political liberals, and local autonomy for political conservatives."[112]

Compare Lovins' promises to those of the young Xhosa prophetess: "There would rise cattle, horses, sheep, goats, dogs, fowls and every other animal that was wanted and all clothes and everything they would wish for to eat the same as English people eat, and all kinds of things for their houses would all come out of the ground."[113]

In a precursor of today's theme of "green jobs," renewables were supposed to replace fossil fuels. Despite his lack of any technical credentials, Earth Day coordinator Denis Hayes was installed in 1979 as director of the Department of Energy's Solar Energy Research Institute. Hayes boldly announced solar could meet 50 percent of U.S. energy needs by the year 2000.[114] Two years later the institute issued a report asserting solar energy and conservation could make the United States wholly energy-independent by the turn of the century.[115] Dismissed by President Ronald Reagan, Hayes went out in a burst of utopian self-righteousness, charging "a gang of mad mullahs" had seized power in Washington.[116]

Meanwhile, leading environmental organizations worked to impede economically viable energy development. While most Americans think of the Sierra Club as an outfit that organizes hikes, its energy program opposed nuclear energy, strip mining of coal, offshore oil drilling, most geothermal operations, and "the sacrifice for water power of any ... high quality scenic resource area."[117] The Natural Resources Defense Council (NRDC), with its army of lawyers, was the most effective, bringing suit against producers of all the major energy sources: nuclear, coal, oil, and hydroelectric.[118]

The Environmental Protection Agency, established by Richard Nixon in December 1970, eight months after Earth Day, would be the most significant institutional product of the environmental apocalypse. EPA promptly used the Clean Air Act and its 1977 amendments to throw up roadblocks against new industry.

The first casualties were two 700 MW coal-fired power plants in Montana, a $1.4 billion project. EPA stepped in on the grounds that its computer-generated air model predicted that on some days each year air quality standards on a Northern Cheyenne Indian reservation miles away might be violated. An EPA spokesman explained, in a position that still characterizes the agency, "economics in a sense becomes irrelevant."[119]

For all their achievements, the environmental roosters were victims of their own success. They had ended any prospect of more nuclear energy. Air pollution levels were down dramatically. The public was becoming complacent, even a little bored. It was difficult to generate excitement over the good news, that last year sulfur dioxide emissions had fallen this much, nitrogen oxide that much.

There was a promising apocalyptic stirring in the mid-1970s. *Time* magazine trumpeted "Another Ice Age?" (1975) and "The Big Freeze" (1977), *Newsweek* lamented "The Cooling World" (1975), and *The Christian Science Monitor* foresaw a "New Ice Age Almost Upon Us" (1979).[120] Just as today, blame was placed on industrial emissions.[121] But the global cooling panic blew over before it really got started. And so, when global warming's waxing wave rose in the late 1980s – to become a monumental breaking wave in the 1990s – environmentalism obtained a huge apocalyptic jolt.

The entire planet was in imminent danger of collapse, we were told, if we did not drastically cut back on our use of energy from fossil fuels. The panic mobilized people, and their governments, on a scale that dwarfed the impact of the first environmentalist wave. The only question was how forcefully to act, not whether there was reason to act at all.

Chapter 5
A Climate Rooster Becomes President

With the election of Barack Obama in 2008, the United States for the first time had a president who identified himself as an unabashed climate rooster.

In January 2009, the administration's first month in office, Secretary of State Hillary Clinton set the apocalyptic tone. Chief among the challenges of the twenty-first century, she said, "is the complex, urgent, and global threat of climate change. From rapidly rising temperatures to melting arctic ice caps, from lower crop yields to dying forests, from unforgiving hurricanes to unrelenting droughts, we have no shortage of evidence that our world is facing a climate crisis. ... Under president Barack Obama, the U.S. will take the lead in addressing this challenge."[122]

One month later, Obama asked Congress for a new energy policy: "To save our planet from the ravages of climate change, we need to ultimately make clean, renewable energy the profitable kind of energy. So I ask this Congress to send me legislation that places a market-based cap on carbon pollution and drives the production of more renewable energy in America."[123] (That legislation was Waxman-Markey, which as we have seen failed to clear the Senate.)

A year later Obama was sounding the same
themes: "Climate change poses a threat to our way of
life. In fact we're already beginning to see its
profound and costly impact."[124] (We were seeing its
effect in the political shutdown of our energy supply,
but of course that's not what Obama meant.) "The
next generation," Obama promised, "will not be held
hostage to energy sources from the last century."[125]

Nor was he open to astonishing information that
might deflect him from his chosen course. Harold
Hamm, billionaire CEO of Continental Resources and
discoverer of the Bakken oil fields of Montana and
North Dakota, attended a White House "giving
summit" for wealthy Americans who had pledged to
donate at least half their wealth to charity. In a *Wall
Street Journal* interview he tells what happened when
it was his turn to talk to President Obama: "I told him
of the revolution in the oil and gas industry and how
we have the capacity to produce enough oil to enable
America to replace OPEC. I wanted to make sure he
knew about this." Obama's reaction? "He turned to
me and said, 'Oil and gas will be important for the
next few years. But we need to go on to green and
alternative energy.'"[126]

Like the Xhosa chief of chiefs Sarhili, who also
ignored warnings, Obama threw the full weight of his
prestige and office behind the apocalypse. For both it
was a risky strategy. Landes notes it made no
"rational" sense for Sarhili and his fellow chiefs to
bind their fate so closely to such a dangerous

prophecy. Nonetheless, Sarhili committed himself, up to and including threats of violence against unbelievers.

Too late Sarhili woke up to the folly of what he had done: "I am no longer a chief. I was a great chief, being as I am the son of Hintza, who left me rich in cattle and people, but I have been deluded into the folly of destroying my cattle and ordering my people to do the same."[127] Obama would mobilize his administration to hobble the production of tried and true fossil fuels upon which our economy depends while encouraging (and subsidizing) the favored forms of green energy, sun and wind, convinced by the global warming "prophets" they were viable substitutes.

Targeting Coal, Oil, Natural Gas

One by one, each major energy source has been specifically targeted by the Obama administration. In the view of global warming apocalyptics, coal, which provides half of our electricity and is the cheapest form of energy – and of which this country has huge reserves – is the worst fuel of them all. Leading rooster James Hansen has called coal "the single greatest threat to civilization and all life on our planet."[128] As a candidate, Obama offered fair warning to those who would develop our coal resources: "If somebody wants to build a coal-powered plant they can; it's just that it will bankrupt them because they're going to be charged a huge sum for all that greenhouse gas that's being emitted."[129]

Under Lisa Jackson, Obama's chosen head of EPA, even existing coal plants are threatened. The most serious of the draconian air quality regulations EPA is using to kill coal plants are the MACT rule (Maximum Achievable Control Technology, in EPA-speak) and the Cross-State Air Pollution Rule. Both of these made House Majority Leader Eric Cantor's list of the top 10 job-killing regulations in America.[130]

The problem with MACT is that much of the technology is not "achievable" because it is either too expensive or nonexistent. American Electric Power, the Tennessee Valley Authority, Dominion Resources, and TransAlta have all said they will have to close down a number of plants.[131] Those that can be saved will have to be retrofitted at enormous cost, to be paid by the consumer in significantly higher electricity rates.

The net result will be to drive up the cost of coal substantially and reduce our energy supply by roughly 81 gigawatts.[132] By way of comparison, the largest solar plant in the world, the planned $2.2 billion Ivanpah Solar Electric Generating System in the Mojave Desert, which will cover 5.6 square miles with mirrors (if it survives various environmentalist challenges), will provide one-half of 1 percent of what is being lost.[133]

The Obama administration also has in its sights oil, which provides almost 40 percent of our total energy. The BP oil spill gave Obama the excuse to shut down all drilling for many months in the Gulf of Mexico – with the Western United States and Alaska thrown in for good measure. The irony here runs deep. BP, apparently convinced by its own slogan that it was Beyond Petroleum, seems to have neglected safety concerns to pour money into green propaganda and the coffers of radical environmental outfits that provided no payback in BP's hour of need.

The Obama administration may designate more than 187,000 square miles in Alaska as critical habitat for polar bears, which environmental groups have been trying to have listed as endangered species although they are not, on the theory that global warming may make them so in the future.[134] Alaskans fear this could make oil and gas production in the state prohibitively expensive.[135]

There are estimated to be 130 million barrels of oil and one trillion cubic feet of natural gas off the Virginia shore, and Gov. Bob McDonnell spoke of making Virginia the "state energy capital of the East Coast." Not so fast, said the Obama administration. The Interior Department insists on years of review before issuing any drilling leases.[136]

Playing games with permits and leases is an excellent method of choking off new oil supplies.

Shell Oil almost threw in the towel when the Interior
Department and EPA, citing fears of global warming,
refused to issue drilling permits after the company
had spent more than $3.5 billion on exploration and
acquiring leases in the Chukchi Sea off the northwest
coast of Alaska.[137] Shell redesigned its drilling plan
and finally received the needed air quality permit, but
that's just the beginning. It must come up with a
satisfactory oil spill response plan, and of course deal
with the inevitable rush of legal challenges by the
environmental lobby.

Conoco Phillips spent five years trying to get a
permit to drill at one of its leases on Alaska's North
Slope, only to be denied in the end.[138] The board of
Royal Dutch Shell has had enough. Shell USA
President Marvin Odum says the board is raising
serious concerns over the political and regulatory risk
attached to investment in the United States.[139]

Exxon has made a huge oil discovery in the Gulf,
the largest since BP's Thunder Horse Field in 1999.
When Exxon applied for an extension of its lease,
normally a routine matter, the Obama administration
denied it based, Exxon said, on legal interpretations
the government "had never before applied and had
never before articulated."[140] Interior Secretary Ken
Salazar also has delayed a 2008 plan to begin
development of rich deposits of oil shale on two
million acres of federal land in Colorado, Utah, and
Wyoming. He wants new environmental requirements
to   be   met.   The   U.S.   Energy   Information

Administration estimates the area holds enough oil to displace all foreign oil imports for several centuries.[141]

The Anti-Fracking Campaign

Following coal and oil, natural gas is our third major source of energy. The effort to shut down its production is also fraught with irony given that it produces significantly less emissions (greenhouse and otherwise) than coal or oil and was touted by environmentalists during their anti-coal campaigns as a "bridge fuel" to the green Eden ahead.[142] The rising use of shale gas has allowed U.S. carbon dioxide emissions to fall by 1.7 percent over the past decade, faster than emissions fell in Europe, with its costly national carbon trading schemes.[143] But as the available supply of natural gas has increased dramatically, thanks to hydraulic fracturing ("fracking") techniques, this once-touted energy source has come into the environmentalists' crosshairs.

Fracking uses pressured water, sand, and trace amounts of chemicals to produce cracks in underground shale rock formations allowing oil or natural gas to be brought to the surface. The technique allows for horizontal drilling, making natural gas and oil deposits accessible from drilling points miles away. In 2004, when few recognized its economic

potential, fracking obtained a clean bill of health from
EPA, which concluded a four-year study by
determining fracking posed "little or no threat to
drinking water." The agency found no warrant for
further study.[144]

Now environmentalists are throwing everything
they can come up with at fracking, hoping something
sticks. The anti-fracking campaign is taking on the
frenzied character of the anti-nuclear energy
campaign of an earlier era. In September 2011, seven
hundred protesters bearing such signs as "Fracking
Poisons Air and Water. Fight Back Now" converged
on the Pennsylvania Convention Center in
Philadelphia, where a shale gas convention was being
held. Reminiscent of the hysteria in the wake of Three
Mile Island, protesters claimed people were falling ill,
cattle dying, and pets losing their hair.[145] *Gasland*, a
copycat scare "documentary" in the tradition of Al
Gore's *An Inconvenient Truth*, warns fracking could
make the water in your faucet flammable,[146] make
your house explode, cause earthquakes, or poison
you.

Although Obama is not responsible for this
hysteria, under his leadership EPA has positioned
itself in the forefront of the scaremongers. With
Congress, under activist pressures, having mandated
another EPA report on the impact of fracking on
drinking water, Kathleen Hartnett White, formerly
chairman of the Texas Commission on Environmental
Quality, writes the study seems designed to

substantiate a predetermined conclusion: that hydraulic fracturing poses grave risks.[147] The report is to be an inside job – the review panel excludes anyone with professional expertise, as they are automatically assumed to be industry shills. Representatives of state regulatory agencies with six decades of experience with fracking are likewise excluded from the report-writing panel, and the researchers, says White, seem unaware of the difference between computer models of the assumed effect of fracking and actual physical measurements of its results.[148]

In July 2011 EPA performed a little jazz of its own by announcing its study would go beyond water to the dangers posed by transport, mixing, delivery, and potential accidents in the fracking process. In other words, something has to stick. The way then will be open to onerous EPA regulation of all drilling that uses fracking, not to mention moratoria while further "studies" are conducted. Lynn Helms, director of North Dakota's Department of Mineral Resources, believes EPA is on track to stop fracking cold for between one and two years in January. That's when state regulators must write new rules for fracking based on an EPA guidance document now under review by the Office of Management and Budget. A similar guidance document issued by EPA for Alabama (following an environmental lawsuit) halted fracking in that state for many months. Helms estimates the expected shutdown will last a minimum of 15 months in North Dakota, "and that's only if we red-lighted everything else and got nothing else done. [149]

The economic cost of a fracking ban? In *Regulators Gone Wild*, Rich Trzupek cites a study by IHS Global Insight, which finds a ban would cost the United States $374 billion in lost GDP by 2014, would result in the loss of about three million jobs, and would require a 60 percent increase in imported oil and natural gas to make up the shortfall. Restrictions, rather than a ban, would produce a $172 billion reduction in GDP, a loss of 1.4 million jobs, and a 30 percent increase in energy imports. [150]

The Obama administration has even recruited the Securities and Exchange Commission (SEC) to help fuel the anti-fracking furor. Its purported rationale? Ensuring "investors are being told about risks a company may face related to its operations, such as lawsuits, compliance costs or other uncertainties." [151]

Putting Energy Exploration Off-Limits

The administration has various methods to attack oil, coal, and gas simultaneously. One way is to make the places energy is found off-limits to exploration and production. Given that the federal government owns so much of the territory of resource-rich Western states – 60 percent of Utah, 30 percent of Montana – this is an effective strategy. In 2010 the federal

Bureau of Land Management halted all oil and natural gas lease sales on federal lands in Montana, North Dakota, and South Dakota while it studies how the leases might contribute to global warming.[152] In 2009 Salazar infuriated Utah's lawmakers by withdrawing 77 leases for oil and gas exploration on federal lands in the state.[153]

There are a raft of tricks up the bureaucratic sleeve. One is wilderness designation. In 2010 Salazar directed the Bureau of Land Management to inventory federal land for "wilderness characteristics," which essentially means almost any excuse could be found to make millions more acres off limits to energy exploration as "wild lands."[154] He had to back down, at least temporarily, when a substantial number of Congressmen protested that only Congress had the right to designate public lands as wilderness areas.[155]

Then there's the 1906 Antiquities Act. Originally designed to protect Indian sites and fossil deposits, it's become a device to cripple energy development,[156] as has the Endangered Species Act. In 2011 residents of the oil-rich Permian basin in West Texas and southeastern New Mexico – which produces 20 percent of our domestic crude oil – were trembling in fear that a three-inch-long sand-dwelling lizard, the dunes sagebrush lizard, might be added to the endangered species list.[157] Doing so could have severely curtailed oil and gas exploration in the 17-county Permian Basin, which new fracking techniques have endowed with huge additional potential.

Doublespeak on Nuclear Energy

After coal, oil, and natural gas, nuclear power plants are our major source of energy, supplying 20 percent of U.S. electricity. Rhetorically the Obama administration supports nuclear power. In 2010 Obama said safe, new nuclear plants were a "necessity" given that nuclear is "the largest source of fuel that produces no carbon emissions."[158] He even linked nuclear energy to sacrosanct sun and wind. "Whether it's nuclear energy or solar or wind energy, if we fail to invest in the technologies of tomorrow, then we are going to be importing these technologies instead of exporting them."[159] But nuclear power is also an energy of yesterday, and the effort to abolish it is what gave the roosters of the original environmental apocalypse their chief mobilizing tool.

The proof Obama is not serious in supporting nuclear power is that he has cancelled further development of the Yucca Mountain repository for nuclear waste in Nevada, in which the U.S. government already had invested $9 billion. In doing so he handed anti-nuclear activists an irrefutable argument: They can object that we cannot create more nuclear waste when we have no long-term repository – or prospect of one – in which to store the nuclear waste we already have. Indeed, a number of states, California among them, forbid the building of any new nuclear plant until a permanent waste repository is in place. We could reprocess the waste as fuel, as many other countries do, but Obama has made no mention of that.

Yet another sign the Obama administration is not serious in promoting nuclear power is Salazar's ban on uranium mining on federal lands in northern Arizona. (The chief civilian use for uranium is to fuel nuclear power plants.) The U.S. Geological Survey estimates the area contains 375 million pounds of high-grade uranium ore, the energy equivalent of 13 billion barrels of oil. In 2009 Salazar announced he was considering withdrawing the land from mining for twenty years and putting new mining claims on hold for two years while his staff studied the issue. In a draft environmental impact statement of more than 1,000 pages, the Interior Department's Bureau of Land Management concluded mining would do little irreparable harm. Never mind. In a move reminiscent of EPA Administrator William Ruckelshaus's banning of DDT after EPA's extensive hearings gave it a clean bill of health, Salazar declared his intention to go ahead with the ban anyway.[160]

In other words, Obama has offered nuclear power nothing more than lip service. Yes, he offered an $8 billion guarantee for nuclear plants that hardy souls still hope to build in Georgia and South Carolina. But even then he made it clear he saw this as a quid pro quo for what he hoped (vainly, as it turned out) would be Republican support for cap-and-trade legislation.[161]

Chapter 6
Pitfalls of Green Energy

The Obama administration's energy policy rules out everything except sun and wind – and there's no doubt of the administration's commitment to these forms of "green energy." In his rousing maiden speech to both houses of Congress in February 2009, Obama pledged to put creating a green economy at the top of the national agenda.[162] But green energy is more a Xhosa-like prophecy of future plenty than a way to fuel our economy.

When it comes to wind energy, an executive of the international utility company EON was blunt: Without government mandates forcing use of renewables, "nobody would be building wind farms."[163] As for solar, which is even more expensive, the government's $500 million "investment" of stimulus funds in Solyndra received massive coverage because of suspected political favoritism and Obama's embarrassing-in-retrospect announcement on his ballyhooed visit to Solyndra that "the future is here."[164] The furor generated by all this obscured the more basic point that even with huge subsidies, companies with products that cannot compete in the marketplace are apt to go under.

The Obama administration's reaction, like that of Sarhili when the prophecy was not fulfilled despite the first wave of cattle-slaughter and crops-burning,

was to double down. In the immediate aftermath of
the Solyndra scandal, the Department of Energy
hastily shoveled out $7.9 billion for clean energy
projects just before stimulus funds ran out.[165] Since,
by the Energy Information Administration's
estimates, solar and wind energy will cost five times
per megawatt hour what a new gas-fired power plant
would cost, the prospects for a long-term return on
"investment" can scarcely be called promising.

There's yet another headwind. Obama, like most
politicians, has taken at face value the environmental
movement's enthusiasm for renewable energy. But
back in the 1970s scientist-writer Peter Metzger
observed environmentalists are enthusiastic for
energy sources as long as they do not exist, and he
predicted hostility to solar power should it become
viable.[166] Those who made of renewables a holy grail
had in mind small-is-beautiful solar panels on the roof
or a small windmill in the backyard – not huge
commercial wind farms and vast arrays of solar
panels with endless miles of transmission towers to
bring their energy to the customer.

The scene is set for growing conflict between
environmental outfits and politicians who think they
are in the forefront of green right-thinking. A
coalition of environmental and Native American
groups brought suit against the Department of the
Interior for approving the huge Ivanpah solar project
and five other smaller solar projects in the California
deserts. In April 2011 building on two-thirds of the

Ivanpah project was halted, at least temporarily, when the U.S Bureau of Land Management found more than 600 desert tortoises could die as a result of construction.[167]

Salazar approved the Cape Wind project on Nantucket Sound, the first offshore wind farm in the United States, proclaiming it in the vanguard of "a clean energy revolution." That didn't deter environmental opponents from filing lawsuits against Cape Wind, charging violations of the Endangered Species Act, National Environmental Policy Act, Outer Continental Shelf Lands Act, tribal protection laws, Clean Water Act, Migratory Bird Treaty Act, and Rivers and Harbors Act.[168] In October 2011 opponents hit paydirt when the Alliance to Protect Nantucket Sound succeeded, at least temporarily, in preventing the project from getting off the ground: A federal appeals court ordered the Federal Aviation Administration to redo its study that had concluded the wind turbines would not affect aircraft safety.[169]

It's too early to tell how the green battle against green energy will play out. Many politicians are roosters, true believers in the global warming apocalypse. They did not anticipate coming into conflict with fellow roosters, especially from the environmental movement whose agenda they thought they pursued. Yet as politicians they also feel the need to produce visible results, in this case big green projects.

In Europe the political class is riding roughshod over protestors. Journalist (and decided owl) Christopher Booker writes that in England more than a hundred local campaigns against wind farms have turned to him for help.[170] But the odds are stacked against them. Even though they win every battle locally, in the end an inspector from London may rule the wind farm must go ahead because it is "government policy." In the United States the array of acts passed in the first phase of the environmental apocalypse – many of them employed against Cape Wind – make opposition more likely to succeed.

The Xhosa realized cattle and crops were the key to their prosperity. Destroying all they had in hopes the ancestors would bring better replacements was a very poor way to maintain that prosperity. Our economic growth and well-being depend on an abundant energy supply. Shackling the energy sources we have for the will o' the wisp of sun and wind is no path to a better future. As *Regulators Gone Wild* author Rich Trzupek says, the only thing solar power achieves is to separate taxpayers from billions of their hard-earned dollars.[171]

Our Growing Energy Resources

The irony is that our domestic energy sources are potentially so abundant we could, if we chose, actually reach what was long thought of as never-never land: energy independence. We could become net exporters of energy. That seems wildly at odds with Obama's standard pitch: "We have less than 2 percent of the world's oil reserves. We need to invest in clean, renewable energy." But as *Eco-Imperialism* author Paul Driessen counters, "We have 2 percent of world oil reserves because we've made most of our resources off limits."[172]

Nor is oil the sole key to a rich energy future. In 1980 economist Julian Simon made a famous bet: He challenged the prediction of biologist and doomsday prophet Paul Ehrlich that severe resource scarcity would inevitably accompany population growth. Inviting Ehrlich to choose any five metals, Simon offered to bet their price would fall over the next ten years. It seemed a slam dunk, and Ehrlich, along with physicist John Holdren and two other scientists, selected chrome, copper, nickel, tin, and tungsten. Although the world's population rose by 800 million in the 1980s, the price of every single one of those metals fell, and not just in inflation-adjusted prices but in actual price.[173] Illustrating the power of fashionable ideas over good ideas, Ehrlich and Holdren both would receive lucrative MacArthur genius awards and Holdren would be appointed energy czar in the Obama administration. Simon would have to be content with a meager check for less than $1,000 for winning the bet.

The prices of those five metals fell because of technological advances and the magic of substitution.

Better refining techniques and new sources of supply reduced the price of chrome and nickel. Aluminum was substituted for tin in making cans, ceramics for tungsten in tools, and fiber optics replaced copper wires.[174] Similarly, technology brings within reach oil that only recently was inaccessible. Deep sea drilling is making huge new oil reserves available worldwide, including off U.S. shores. Improved hydraulic fracturing techniques unlock vast new domestic oil and gas resources.

Substituting one form of energy for another is also a key to expanding supply. Arthur Robinson – professor of chemistry, editor of *Access to Energy*, and fan of nuclear energy – offers one avenue to energy plenty.[175] Currently 104 nuclear power reactors produce 19 percent of U.S. electricity. Robinson writes that the Palo Verde nuclear power station near Phoenix, with three reactors, was supposed to have ten, the remaining seven falling victim to the panic the first wave of environmentalists generated. If one station of ten plants on the original Palo Verde model were to be built in each state, those stations could meet all U.S. electricity needs, with plenty to spare for export.

Robinson estimates the admittedly high construction costs could be repaid in just a few years by savings on what's now spent for foreign oil and by income from exported energy. Once up and running, operating costs for nuclear plants are very low. As for nuclear waste, Robinson says the United States should reprocess spent nuclear fuel (as Canada, England, France, Japan, and Russia do), which would eliminate the need for a storage facility for high-level nuclear waste.[176]

That is only one scenario. The real energy revolution (as distinct from the spurious "green revolution") is the potential of natural gas from shale to transform U.S. energy production. As recently as 2000, shale gas constituted 1 percent of U.S. gas supplies. Today it is 25 percent.[177] Virtually overnight the United States has overtaken Russia to become the world's largest producer of natural gas.

The plentiful supply, which has driven down prices, is prompting major companies to develop alternative uses for natural gas so as to boost demand. Eighteen-wheel trucks, with their heavy use of fuel, are an obvious target, but the problem is the high cost of conversion and the need for fueling stations. So the search is on for methods to convert natural gas into a fuel that could work in existing vehicles. Chesapeake Energy is investing in technologies to create a new natural gas-based fuel that could work in existing gasoline engines,[178] as is South Africa-based chemical giant Sasol, which announced plans to build a $10 billion plant in Louisiana to convert natural gas into diesel fuel to power cars and trucks.[179]

It's worth noting the genuine positive feedback from new energy sources. A new $650 million steel plant – unthinkable a few years ago – is being built in Youngstown, Ohio, close to the Marcellus shale deposits, to make the steel tubes used in fracking.[180] Exploration for shale gas – a huge steel consumer – has persuaded other steelmakers to expand in the area. Since steelmakers are heavy users of natural gas, cheap gas allows them to become competitive despite cheaper labor abroad.[181]

Plentiful natural gas is also revitalizing the chemistry industry. In 2010, industry exports increased nearly 20 percent, shifting the industry's balance of trade from a $100 million deficit to a $3.7 billion surplus.[182]

Europe Pays a Heavy Price

That any shortage of energy from which we may suffer is artificial and politically induced will make it no less painful. In Europe the damage is more advanced than it is here, because European countries have made the biggest investment in the quixotic attempt to freeze the climate of the globe at some arbitrarily determined ideal temperature.

In an interview with CNN's Piers Morgan on September 19, 2011, Norway's prime minister, Jens Stoltenberg, said he looked upon the actions his country and others were taking to reduce greenhouse gas emissions as an "insurance policy," just in case the catastrophic predictions were right. But people who take out insurance aren't apt to buy policies whose annual premiums are higher than the total damage any rational risk-evaluator could tell them they might conceivably suffer far in the future.

In England, the government has released its estimates of the sums it would take to ring the coasts with huge offshore wind farms. The estimate is £140 billion, which works out to £5,600 for every household in the country – $8,972 in U.S. dollars. Conventional sources could provide the same amount of energy at 5 percent of the cost.[183] That's self-sacrifice not quite on the order of the Xhosas, but it's up there.

Worse still, rolling blackouts are in the cards for both England and Germany and if the Socialists have their way, even in France. After Fukushima, France – whose 58 nuclear facilities provide 75 percent of its electricity – is wobbling in its forty-year commitment to nuclear energy. Francois Hollande, who won the primary contest to become the Socialist candidate for president, has promised to reduce the country's reliance on nuclear power by one-third. His defeated rival, Martine Aubry, had promised to eliminate nuclear altogether. She offered a bizarre tribute to the industry she would shut down: "We must use the excellence of our nuclear industry to ... dismantle nuclear plants."[184]

Booker points out England is planning to close 14 nuclear and coal-fired power stations currently supplying nearly 40 percent of its peak electricity needs. Germany, post-Fukushima, has decided to shut down eight of its 17 nuclear power plants immediately, with the rest to follow. Although Germany has the tallest and most powerful wind turbines in the world, even the 6 percent of the nation's electricity they supply is so unreliable the Germans say they need to build new coal-powered plants to back them up.

Given all this, the head of Germany's national grid warned power cuts might be inevitable.[185] Should France – which, along with Czechoslovakia, is making up the shortfall in Germany's energy supply[186] – shut down a number of its own nuclear plants, prospects for keeping the lights on grow even dimmer.

Spain has become the poster child for economic self-mutilation on the climate change altar. Its heavy investment in green energy – which Obama has cited repeatedly as a model for the United States to follow – has caused electricity prices to skyrocket and devastated Spanish industry. That's the finding of a leaked internal assessment by the former Zapatero administration.[187] That assessment notes the price of electricity determines the competitiveness of Spanish industry; the price of electricity had risen to 17 percent above the European average; and the chief reason was the cost of renewables, with government subsidies having increased fivefold between 2004 and 2010.

Christopher Horner of the Competitive Enterprise Institute, who provided excerpts from the leaked report on the Pajamas Media Web site, says the assessment, a government perspective on a flagship program, soft-pedaled its conclusions – the government had moved "too fast" on solar. Nonetheless, the report "reveals that even the socialist Spanish government now acknowledges the ruinous effects of green economic policy."[188] Not long after that internal assessment, Bloomberg news reported the Spanish government, seeking to avoid the fate of Greece, "is lancing an 18 billion-euro ($24 billion) investment bubble in solar energy that has boosted public liabilities."[189]

U.S. Follows in Europe's Wake

We are not far behind Europe. If anti-nuclear activists backed by New York Gov. Andrew Cuomo (D) succeed in shutting down Indian Point, studies conducted separately by Charles River Associates (commissioned by the New York City Department of Environmental Protection) and the New York Building Congress warn New York City could experience price spikes and blackouts.[190]

According to a *Wall Street Journal* editorial, a confidential 2010 report issued by the Federal Energy Regulatory Commission estimated EPA regulations would ultimately shut down a large share of U.S. coal-fired plants, resulting in a loss of as much as 8 percent of U.S. electric capacity.[191] As the *Journal* editorial notes, the electric grid is local, so even subtracting a small plant could lead to regional blackouts. That's because the older and less-efficient coal plants slated for closure are often the crucial nodes that connect the hubs and spokes of the grid. If these are taken out, the power system becomes less stable and more difficult to manage and may not be able to meet peak-load demand or unexpected disturbances.[192] In October 2011, 11 governors wrote to EPA protesting its new "utility rule," warning "full time-power availability could be at risk."[193]

As for what is to replace the roughly 81 gigawatts EPA plans to take offline, presumably it's what Dan Kish of the Institute for Energy Research calls "government-funded pixie dust" – sun and wind.[194]

Chapter 7
Confronting Global Warming Roosters

If we are to shift course before worse damage is done, more political owls will have to confront the global warming roosters. Behind the scenes there may well be a number of Senators and Congressmen who clap Sen. James Inhofe (R-Okla.) and Reps. Jim Sensenbrenner (R-Wis.) and Dana Rohrabacher (R-CA) on the back, telling them to keep up the good work, but such owls aren't speaking up.

Inhofe, who has called man-made global warming "the greatest hoax ever perpetrated on the American people" and held hearings airing the views of dissenters – unlike alarmist-dominated hearings, largely ignored by the media – comes from oil-rich Oklahoma, so his frontal assault on the climate change roosters has not hurt him.

For most politicians it requires political courage to take on the roosters at this stage of the apocalypse. When Texas Gov. Rick Perry challenged climate change dogma, *New York Times* chief pundit Thomas Friedman called him "crazy,"[195] and former President Bill Clinton was disdainful: "You can't win the nomination of a major political party in the U.S. unless you deny science?"[196] Such reactions show the roosters still control the discourse on climate change. It's not deemed necessary to argue the case with the

dissenting owls – a leading media figure and a
prominent political figure both deem derision a
sufficient response. And derision is not something
politicians relish.

The public is beginning to tire of the hysteria.
Public anxiety peaked in 2007. Gone are the days
when an Argentine couple (Francisco Lotero and
Miriam Coletti) would shoot themselves and two of
their children in a suicide pact over fear of the effects
of global warming.[197] A February 7, 2010 BBC poll
found only 26 percent of the British public believed in
man-made global warming,[198] an astonishing collapse,
especially given the BBC's nonstop propaganda
barrage on the need for immediate action to ward off
Armageddon.

A January 5, 2010 Pew poll found global warming
ranked dead last among 21 options for action by the
president and Congress, four points below the
next-lowest priority, trade policy.[199] A July 2011
Harris poll found only 44 percent of Americans polled
believed carbon dioxide emissions were warming the
Earth, down from 71 percent in 2007.[200] A month
later a Nielsen poll found 48 percent of Americans
were concerned about climate change, a drop of 14
percentage points from 2007.[201]

Scientific opinion, always divided, is shifting. For
those willing to go beyond sound bites, puncturing the
global warming balloon may be easier than it seems.
The owls have all the backup needed to make their
case. There is now a large body of scientific work

challenging the thesis of catastrophic man-made global warming. *Climate Change Reconsidered*, the 2009 report of the Nongovernmental International Panel on Climate Change (NIPCC), summarized thousands of scientific studies refuting claims made by the IPCC's *Fourth Assessment Report*.[202] *Climate Change Reconsidered* was followed in 2011 by a 430-page *Interim Report* including more recent scientific studies.

There are also excellent books for laymen, such as Steve Goreham's *Climatism*, Larry Bell's *Climate of Corruption*, and Fred Singer and Dennis Avery's *Unstoppable Global Warming*. There is The Heartland Institute's monthly newspaper, *Environment & Climate News*. Since 2008 Heartland has hosted six international conferences on climate change bringing together thousands of prominent scientists and policy experts. Presentations delivered at these conferences are available online at *climateconference.heartland.org*. There are dissenting petitions and statements signed by hundreds – in some cases thousands – of scientists.

There are scores of Web sites, including Climate Depot, Climate Change Reconsidered, Power for USA, Science and Environmental Policy Project, and ClimateWiki. There's the 2007 film *The Great Global Warming Swindle*, which appeared on Great Britain's Channel 4. Although a much better documentary than Gore's *An Inconvenient Truth* (it provided the inconvenient truths Gore omitted), it had nothing like the impact. Indeed, not a single U.S. television channel picked it up.

As electricity bills go up, public enthusiasm for action to stave off climate change goes down, as does the enthusiasm of government leaders who had seen green policies as gold at the ballot box and now are shocked at the prospect they might lead to electoral defeat – that indeed pursuing those policies might mean they would find themselves, like Sarhili, chiefs no longer. Although only last year U.K. Prime Minister David Cameron promised his would be "the greenest government ever," in October George Osborne, chancellor of the exchequer, stunned delegates to the Tory party's national conference by saying forthrightly, "We're not going to save the planet by putting our country out of business."[203]

The European Union is showing some early signs of rethinking its commitment to far-reaching emissions reductions beyond Kyoto. In an internal memo obtained by Dow Jones Newswires, the Energy Department of the European Commission observes, "there is a trade-off between climate-change policies and competitiveness."[204] Translation: Kyoto, with its 5 percent emissions reduction target, is killing us. What will happen if we follow the program and bring down emissions – as we are mandated to do – by 20 percent in 2020, with reductions of 80 to 95 percent proposed for 2050? By the E.U.'s own estimate, the cost of meeting that relatively modest 5 percent target comes to at least $67 billion a year.

If other countries don't also cripple themselves with emission reduction targets – and there is little indication they will do so[205] – the Energy Department suggests the E.U. should reconsider whether to switch its domestic energy base away from carbon-emitting sources.[206] Like the Xhosa, the Europeans have decided everybody has to participate for the sacrifice to have the promised effect. But whereas this conviction doomed the Xhosa as roosters destroyed the property of recalcitrant owls, it could save Europe.[207]

As Landes notes, eventually the apocalyptic booster rocket gives out. The great breaking wave is followed by the broken wave as the signs cease to appear, the converts grow fewer, defections grow. Sometimes there is a defining moment – it's probable the Climategate scandal will turn out to have served that role in the global warming apocalypse. Eventually, inexorable time gives victory to the owls.

Given this prospect, political leaders not swept up by the successive waves will be tempted to wait them out, rather than speak up and take politically dangerous flack from enraged roosters. But waiting patiently until the climate change apocalypse reaches its inevitable end carries its own dangers. There's no predicting when that will happen, and our economy, like that of the Xhosa, could be left in ruins. It will then be cold comfort that the atmospheric physicist and MIT meteorology professor Richard Lindzen was prophetic when he said, "Future generations will wonder in bemused amazement that the early twenty-first century's developed world went into hysterical panic over a globally averaged temperature increase of a few tenths of a degree, and, on the basis of gross exaggerations of highly uncertain computer projections combined into implausible chains of inference proceeded to contemplate a rollback of the industrial age."[208]

The longer the apocalyptic wave continues, the more difficult it is to undo the damage. So much has been invested, the programs and institutions go forward on their own momentum. Cap and trade becomes a source of tax revenue governments do not want to give up. The reason the program was instituted is long forgotten, but the tax goes on. New reasons can be found to continue mandates in which there has been heavy financial investment – for example, a slogan like "energy independence" can replace "global warming" in order to pour still more money into wind and sun. Even when the roosters fall silent, we could still be using wildly expensive politically sanctified forms of energy that produce only a tiny proportion of what is needed while the political tourniquet remains on the exploration and production of the real energy we have in abundance.

Taking on the Environmental Movement

The really hard part is not taking on global warming, but taking on the environmental movement. If we are to develop our energy resources, owls must defeat the roosters of the underlying apocalypse of which, as we noted earlier, global warming is only a riff.

The environmental movement has grown into a colossus, with huge financial resources from membership dues, fund appeals, and foundation, corporate, and government funding. To take just two of the many such organizations, the Sierra Club has an annual budget of $83 million, the Natural Resources Defense Council $80 million, with most of the latter's budget devoted to lawyers. It is no wonder few relish the prospect of tangling with the environmental lobby and its reflexive media allies.

Compounding the problem, the public has a warm fuzzy feeling about environmentalists as people who are against pollution and want to save polar bears and natural habitats. Many will find it difficult to accept that those who set the agenda for the movement are opposed to all large-scale energy production. The public assumes they are for clean energy, not a lot less energy.

Who, after all, thinks the Xhosa are in our midst? Obviously New York City's Mayor Bloomberg hasn't a clue – he has given $50 million to the Sierra Club's campaign to shut down coal plants.[209] Few environmental leaders are as candid as Maurice

Strong, longtime head of the United Nations Environment Programme and organizer of the 1992 Rio Earth Summit, who said at that conference, "We may get to the point where the only way of saving the world will be for industrial civilization to collapse."[210]

Because the environmentalists have been able to play their game unchallenged for so long, making the case against them now is difficult. But if we don't succeed, when the inevitable blackouts and energy rationing and sky-high bills come, it is the energy and utility companies that will be blamed for shortages and overcharging. The environmental groups, which are the real villains, will be leading the virtuous charge ... and getting away with it.

Of course, punishing the corporate victims for the sins of the accusers will only further reduce our energy supply. Meanwhile, the environmentalists will be on to the next best thing. If the man-made global warming wave has receded by then, the environmental roosters will have manufactured another crisis du jour. Ocean "acidification," perhaps, or – don't laugh – back to global cooling. Whatever it is, you can be sure it's man-made and requires severe limits on energy use.

If the environmental lobby is not overcome, little will change. Even presidents who would like to encourage energy production come up against an alphabet soup of agencies armed with a vast number of "Acts" passed over several decades by careless

Congresses. The bureaucrats running these agencies are largely responsible for writing environmental laws, which they are free to interpret as they see fit and implement with the full force of law.

As Mark Steyn observes, "right-of-center parties will once in a while be in office, but never in power, merely presiding over vast left-wing bureaucracies that cruise on regardless."[211] President George W. Bush was not even able to get drilling in a tiny, nondescript portion of the Arctic National Wildlife Refuge, let alone make inroads in the environmental bureaucracies he in theory directed.

Those who have made inroads in these bureaucracies are roosters from the major groups behind the environmental apocalypse. Agencies that play a role in regulating energy use – premier among them the Environmental Protection Agency and Department of the Interior – are riddled with activists who came from outfits like the Natural Resources Defense Council, Friends of the Earth, and Sierra Club.

The movement of personnel goes both ways, as regulators move into the major environmental groups, bringing with them valuable knowledge about how the agencies work. Now that an especially friendly administration has come in – there's never been anything like Obama's – environmental groups have experienced a genuine, if temporary brain drain, as their leaders have moved en masse to Washington to

take top posts in the agencies most important to them
and to shape policy at the White House.[212]

Transforming the Climate of Opinion

The prerequisite to political change is a change of
public consciousness. Although Nobel Laureate
economist Milton Friedman was referring to a
different issue, what he said applies precisely to
environmentalism: "I do not believe that the answer
to our problem is simply to elect the right people. The
important thing is to establish a political climate of
opinion which will make it politically profitable for
the wrong people to do the right thing. Unless it is
politically profitable for the wrong people to do the
right thing, the right people will not do the right thing
either, or if they try, they will shortly be out of
office."[213]

Suppose, in the present political climate of
opinion, a Republican president – even if both houses
of Congress had a Republican majority – were to call
for abolishing EPA and turning over its functions to
the states, each of which have their own
environmental agencies. Rich Trzupek is undoubtedly
correct when he writes in *Regulators Gone Wild*, "the
hyperbole and hysteria from the left would be
deafening if such an attempt were made."[214]

Ironically, the corporate victims, as Trzupek
writes, bear part of the responsibility for the extent to

which environmentalism has become ingrained in our culture.[215] British Petroleum, with its pretense that its initials stand for Beyond Petroleum, may have gone to the outer reaches of absurdity, but hundreds of corporations have based their ad campaigns on how "green" they are.

For all the difficulty, we are aided in the task by the very overreaching of EPA. In the name of the innocuous-sounding phrase "sustainable development," EPA is currently engaged in a breathtaking new power grab. In August 2011 the National Academies of Sciences released a report by the National Research Council that had been commissioned by EPA (cost: $700,000) outlining how EPA could integrate "sustainability" into its regulatory responsibilities.[216] Its most horrifying finding: Nothing interferes with EPA's taking on this role. There's no need for Congressional action. According to the report, the National Environmental Policy Act of 1969 provided all the authority EPA needs when it declared it was national policy "to create and maintain conditions under which man and nature can exist in productive harmony, and fulfill the social, economic and other requirements of present and future generations of Americans."[217] Thus do the broad, vague mandates issued by an imprudent Congress do their mischief decades later.

So what is sustainable development? The U.N.'s International Environmental Forum has identified no fewer than 1,000 distinct definitions.[218] The NAS report offers one: "to create and maintain conditions, under which humans and nature can exist in productive harmony, that permit fulfilling the social, economic, and other requirements of present and future generations."[219] Note that "future generations." EPA is going to issue regulations on today's public based on what it considers "sustainable development" for unlimited "future generations."

In practice, sustainable development is whatever EPA bureaucrats say it is. There's no need for EPA to bother with the scientific measurements involved in pollution control. The National Research Council report raises a number of issues that go under the rubric of sustainability: population growth, widening gaps between rich and poor, depletion of finite natural resources, biodiversity loss, women's rights, climate change and clean energy, disruption of nutrient cycles, sustainable transport, public health, how to control unsustainable patterns of production and consumption (i.e., the way we live now). Shades of a previous (happily defunct) all-embracing system of central control, the NAS report even talks of three- and five-year plans.[220]

In short, EPA is staking out its right to regulate everything we do, on the ecological principle that "everything is connected to everything else."[221]

Even before this latest power play, EPA's "regulators gone wild" had alienated Congressional Republicans and Democrats alike, who have been pushing back at some of its recent blizzard of regulations.

Also, hard times, however unfortunate in other respects, work in favor of those who would change fundamentally the public's perceptions of the environmental movement. Mark Steyn quotes HarperCollins editor Adam Bellow's comment about Americans having "a certain blithe assurance about the permanence of freedom."[222] This comment is equally true if we substitute "prosperity" for freedom. In bad times, that blithe assurance dissipates.

Energy development brings large numbers of high-paying jobs and lots of money into federal coffers. The proposed Keystone XL pipeline from Alberta to the Gulf Coast was expected to be the source of 20,000 "shovel ready" construction jobs, 118,000 indirect new jobs.[223] The State Department – whose approval was required because the pipeline would cross the 49th parallel, the border between Canada and the U.S. – gave it a thumbs-up after its multi-volume environmental impact statements concluded the pipeline would have "no significant impacts" on the environment.[224] But it has been vociferously opposed by the usual suspects (Greenpeace, the Sierra Club, Environmental Defense, Natural Resources Defense Council, Friends of the Earth), and in November Obama kicked the can down the road to at least 2013, well past the next election. But while Obama may have succeeded in firming up his green constituency, he has done so at the risk of alienating his union supporters, who have spoken up sharply against the decision. To quote Terry O'Sullivan, president of the Laborers' International Union of North America, "The administration chose to support environmentalists over jobs – job-killers win, American workers lose."[225]

Energy consultancy Wood Mackenzie estimates pro-energy development policies could "support an additional 1.4 million jobs and raise over $800 billion of cumulative additional government revenue" by 2030.[226] Make the average person in a faltering economy understand the choice is between driving his car and running his dishwasher and washing machine at a price he can pay and preserving some maybe-endangered lizard in the Permian basin, and there's not much doubt which he'll choose.

Moreover, there is a base of support for taking on the environmental lobby. For at least a decade a number of states have been trying to fight back, thus far with limited success. In 2001, 13 Western states adopted resolutions calling for an end "to EPA's regulatory train wreck."[227] In September 2011 Kansas and Texas, followed by six other states, sued EPA over the Cross-State Air Pollution Rule, which, they charged, would force power providers to implement expensive new technology and purchase power from out of state, and impel existing power plants to shut down. The Brattle Group economic consulting firm estimated the rule would cost consumers up to

$120 billion and reduce the nation's power supply by close to 4 percent.[228]

Western states have been especially incensed over what they see as Washington's land grab. Recently the Utah legislature demanded the national government refrain from designating new land as "national monuments" (another device to keep land off-limits for energy) without the consent of the affected state's legislature. In 2003, Montana pioneered legislation forbidding state land from being sold to the federal government.

Since then, both Utah and Montana have gone further, giving themselves the authority to use eminent domain to seize federal lands and open them up for energy production. Under no illusion where this is headed, the Utah legislature set aside $3 million for the state to counter challenges to the new law in the courts.[229] And in Malta, Montana, more than 2,000 people showed up to protest a Bureau of Land Management scheme (someone had leaked the documents to congressional Republicans) to use the Antiquities Act to give 2.5 million acres national monument status – thus making them out of bounds to energy development. Robert Smith of the Competitive Enterprise Institute says, "Western states are now trying to loosen the shackles of Washington's green serfdom."[230]

The stakes could not be higher. Landes points out that just because the apocalypse is wrong does not mean its effects are not profound. In the case of the

Xhosa, the beneficiaries of the false apocalypse were the British, the very people the Xhosa thought they were expelling through their sacrifice. It was the British who took over the lands the Xhosa could no longer cultivate. China, which is heavily investing in the energy we spurn, is the most probable beneficiary of our folly. How ironic it will be if, despite our pride in bringing down the Soviet Union without a shot, the twenty-first century, thanks to our self-destructive pursuit of an apocalyptic fantasy, belongs to a Communist dictatorship.

About the Author

Rael Jean Isaac has a B.A. from Barnard College (summa cum laude), an M.A. from Johns Hopkins in English literature, and a Ph.D. from the City University of New York in sociology.

She is the author of six books, including *Israel Divided* (Johns Hopkins University Press), *The Coercive Utopians*, with Erich Isaac (Regnery Gateway), *Harvest of Injustice* (National Legal and Policy Center), and *Madness in the Streets*, with Virginia Armat (The Free Press).

She has written on public policy issues for many journals, including *The American Spectator*, *Commentary*, *Midstream*, *The Atlantic*, *National Review*, *The New Republic*, *Conservative Judaism*, *Reader's Digest*, *Chronicles of Culture*, *Politique Internationale*, *Quadrant* (Australia), *The Spectator* (London), *Society*, *Women's Independent Forum*, *Middle East Review*, *The Wall Street Journal*, *The New York Times*, *Cornell Journal of Law and Public Policy*, and *American Enterprise*.

She has four sons and five grandchildren and lives with her husband in Westchester County, New York.

About
The Heartland Institute

The Heartland Institute is a national nonprofit organization with offices in Chicago and Washington, DC. Founded in 1984, it has policy advisors and supporters in all 50 states. Approximately 120 academics and professional economists participate in its peer review process, and more than 200 elected officials serve on its Legislative Forum. Heartland currently has a full-time staff of 41 and a 2012 budget of $7 million.

Heartland contacts more elected officials, more often, than any other think tank in the United States. According to a telephone survey of randomly selected state and local officials conducted in 2011, 79 percent of state legislators and 66 percent of local officials say they read at least one Heartland publication. Heartland's full-time staff of government relations professionals interacts daily with hundreds of elected officials across the country, and its public relations and media specialists help shape public opinion by writing and placing dozens of letters to the editor and opinion editorials each week.

For more information, visit our Web site at www.heartland.org, call 312/377-4000, or write to The Heartland Institute, One South Wacker Drive #2740, Chicago, Illinois 60606.

Endnotes

1. Richard Landes, *Heaven on Earth: The Varieties of the Millennial Experience* (New York, NY: Oxford University Press, 2011), p. 91.

2. Quoted in Rael Jean Isaac and Erich Isaac, *The Coercive Utopians* (Chicago, IL: Regnery, 1983), p. 69.

3. Richard Landes, *supra* note 1, p. 98.

4. *Ibid.*, pp. 97–98.

5. Quoted in Steve Goreham, *Climatism! Science, Common Sense, and the 21st Century's Hottest Topic* (New Lenox, IL: New Lenox Books, 2010), p. 181.

6. Quoted in *ibid.*, p. 16

7. The American Association for the Advancement of Science, National Academy of Sciences, National Oceanic and Atmospheric Administration, National Aeronautics and Space Administration, American Meteorological Society, and American Physical Society are among the scientific organizations in the United States that have formally endorsed the movement. See Goreham, *supra* note 5, p. 17.

8. *Ibid.*, pp. 7–8, 12.

9. Quoted in *ibid.*, p. 12.

10. The actual number was $106.7 billion. *Climate Change: Improvements Needed to Clarify National Priorities and Better Align Them with Federal Funding Decisions*, GAO-11-317, May 20, 2011, http://www.gao.gov/products/GAO-11-317 pdf: http://www.gao.gov/new.items/d11317.pdf Appendix II (p. 48).

11. Goreham, supra note 5, pp. 189–90.

12. Larry Bell, *Climate of Corruption: Politics and Power Behind the Global Warming Hoax* (Austin, TX: Greenleaf Book Group Press, 2011), p. 138.

13. Marianne Lavelle, "The Climate Change Lobby Explosion," February 25, 2009, http://www.iwatchnews.org/node/4593.

14. Bell, *supra* note 12, p. 15.

15. Goreham, *supra* note 5, p. 379.

16. *Ibid.*, p. 100.

17. *Ibid.*, p. 11.

18. "Aliens Could Attack Earth to End Global Warming, NASA Scientist Frets," August 19, 2011, http://www.foxnews.com/scitech/2011/08/19/ aliens-could-attack-earth-to-end-global-warming-nasa-scientist-claims/.

19. Landes, *supra* note 1, pp. 111–19.

20. Goreham, *supra* note 5, pp. 197–98; "Al Gore: Global Warming Skeptics Should Be Shunned Like Racists," August 28, 2011, http://pjmedia.com/tatler/2011/08/28/al-gore-global-warming-skeptics-should-be-shunned-like-racists/.

21. Bell, *supra* note 12, p. 96.

22. Goreham, *supra* note 5, p. 10.

23. *Ibid.*, pp. 217–222. In November 2011, an additional 5,000 files of email correspondence from the world's top climate scientists were anonymously leaked onto the Internet, presumably by the same person or persons who released the first set. Termed in *The Wall Street Journal* Climategate 2.0, this correspondence reveals more chicanery and political activism by the lead scientists who shape the IPCC reports, and a lot more uncertainty about anthropogenic warming theory than these scientists admit in public. James Delingpole, "Climategate 2.0," *The Wall Street Journal*, November 28, 2011.

24. *Ibid.*, p. 222.

25. Bell, *supra* note 12, p. 92.

26. *Ibid.*, p. 93.

27. Frederick Seitz, "A Major Deception on Global Warming," *The Wall Street Journal*, June 12, 1996, http://stephenschneider.stanford.edu/ Publications/PDF_Papers/WSJ_June12.pdf.

28. Bell, *supra* note 12, p. 93.

29. In a December 10, 2009 whitewash of Climategate, FactCheck.org (a project of the Annenberg Foundation) accuses Santer of "bad form" in making a crack about "beat[ing] the crap out of" skeptic Patrick Michaels. http://factcheck.org/2009/12/climategate/.

30. *Climate Change Reconsidered: The Report of the Nongovernmental International Panel on Climate Change* (Chicago: Heartland Institute, 2009), p. iv.

31. Rael Jean Isaac, "A Review of an Important New Report: Climate Change Reconsidered," http://www.familysecuritymatters.org/publications/id.3846/pub_ detail.asp.

32. Donna Laframboise, *The Delinquent Teenager Who Was Mistaken for the World's Top Climate Expert*, 2011, available from Amazon or digital editions by IvyAvenue.com, 2011.

33. Landes, *supra* note 1, pp. 116–19.

34. Goreham, *supra* note 5, p. 381.

35. *Ibid.*, p. 180.

36. Richard A. Muller "The Case Against Global Warming Skepticism," *The Wall Street Journal* (Europe), October 21, 2011. D.J. Keenan has provided a critical statistical analysis of the BEST papers, arguing they use a simplistic and inappropriate statistical model and smooth data, a statistical no-no. Keenan's criticisms and Muller's reply can be found at

http://bishophill.squarespace.com/blog/2011/10/21/keenans-res
ponse-to-the-best-paper.html.

37. Muller, *ibid.*

38. Brad Plumer, "A Skeptical Physicist Ends Up Confirming
Climate Data," *The Washington Post*, October 20, 2011.

39. Ian Semple, "Global Warming Study Finds No Grounds for
Climate Sceptics' Concerns," *The Guardian*, October 20, 2011.

40. Mike Hulme, *Why We Disagree About Climate Change*
(Cambridge, UK: Cambridge University Press, 2009). The book
should be titled *Why We Disagree About* What to Do About
Climate Change, as Hulme ignores the arguments of scientists
skeptical of man-made global warming: The disagreements he
explores are between those who would use market
mechanisms to fight global warming and "deep ecologists" who
believe nothing can be achieved before capitalism is abolished.

41. Hulme defines "normal science" as that guided by Merton's
four classical norms of scientific practice: skepticism,
universalism, communalism, disinterestedness.

42. Hulme, supra note 40, p. 78.

43. According to Hulme, the urgent decisions required by
climate change mean policy makers don't have the luxury of
nonchalance. They must rely on "Bayesian statements,"
informed judgments about likelihoods in the subjective opinion
of well-qualified persons, and consensus, a viewpoint reached
by a group as a whole, usually by majority. *Ibid.*, pp. 81–87.

44. *Ibid.*, p. 326.

45. *Ibid.*

46. For a full discussion of the owls' arguments, see Arthur
Robinson, Noah E. Robinson, and Willie Soon, "Special
Report: Environmental Effects of Increased Atmospheric
Carbon Dioxide," *Environment & Climate News*, January 2008,

http://heartland.org/policy-documents/environmental-effects-inc
reased-atmospheric-carbon-dioxide.

47. Bill McKibben, *Eearth* (New York, NY: Henry Holt, 2010),
pp. 19–20. The odd spelling is to signify the damage to our
Earth is already so great that our world has come to an end
although we don't know it yet.

48. Anne Jolis "The Other Climate Theory," *The Wall Street
Journal*, September 7, 2011.

49. *Climate Change Reconsidered*, supra note 30, p. 11.

50. Roy Spencer and William Braswell, "On the Misdiagnosis of
Surface Temperature Feedbacks from Variations in Earth's
Radiant Energy Balance," *Remote Sensing* 3: 1601–1613, July
25, 2011, http://www.mdpi.com/2072-4292/3/8/1603/pdf.

51. William Gray, "Correcting an MIT Professor's Climate
Errors," *Environment & Climate News*, May 2010.

52. Thomas Opel, Diedrich Fritzsche, Hanno Meyer, Rainer
Schütt, Karin
Weiler, Urs Ruth, Frank Wilhelms, and Hubertus Fischer, "15-
year ice-core data from Akademii Nauk ice cap, Severnaya
Zemlya: high-resolution record of Eurasian Arctic climate
change," *Journal of Glaciology* (2009) 55: 21–31,
epic.awi.de/18879/1/Ope2008c.pdf.

53. Bell, *supra* note 12, p. 233.

54. *Ibid.*, p. 232.

55. Goreham, *supra* note 5, p. 148.

56. *Ibid.*, p. 151.

57. Rudolf Kipp, "The Medieval Warm Period – A global
phenomenon, unprecedented warming, or unprecedented date
manipulation?" http//WattsUpWithThat.com/2009/11/29.

58. Liu Yu, Cai WuiFang, Song Hui Ming, An Zhi Sheng, and Hans W. Linderholm, "Amplitudes, rates, periodicities and causes of temperature variations in the past 2485 years and future trends over the central-eastern Tibetan plateau," *Chinese Science Bulletin*, October 2011 56 (28–29): 2986–94.

59. For an analysis of the benign effects of global warming, see Robinson, Robinson, and Soon, *supra* note 46.

60. John Coleman, Foreword to Goreham, *supra* note 5, p. x.

61. Quoted in *ibid.*, p. 122.

62. *Ibid.*, pp. 172–73.

63. Douglas B. Kell, "Breeding crop plants with deep roots: their role in sustainable carbon, nutrient and water sequestration," *Annals of Botany*, August 3 2011.

64. Quoted in Richard Landes, *supra* note 1, pp. 55–56.

65. *Ibid.*, pp. 52–61.

66. George Will, "Everyone Out of the Water!," *Newsweek*, November 6, 2009.

67. Bell, *supra* note 12, pp. 126–27.

68. *Ibid.*, p. 133; Hal Weitzman, "Political climate looks favourable for Sandor's CCX," *Financial Times*, January 12, 2009, http://www.ft.com/intl/cms/s/0/75da4632-e0ea-11dd-b0e8-0000 77b07658.html#axzz1dtQ8iY8F (registration/subscription required).

69. Bell, *supra* note 12, p. 141.

70. *Ibid.*, p. 140.

71. *Ibid.*, pp. 134-35.

72. Goreham, *supra* note 5, p. 359.

73. Although the two Indian Point nuclear reactors provide 12 percent of the state of New York's electric power and 30 percent of the power used by New York City and Westchester County, Gov. Andrew Cuomo has aligned himself with those trying to shut down the reactors. He said, "The replacement power issue is not a justification to keep Indian Point operating." Neither, apparently, is the far greater cost of any replacement power. See "Cuomo's Indian Point Hype," unsigned, *New York Post*, September 27, 2011.

74. Frede Vestergaard, "Denmark, holder of the next EU Presidency, goes for 100% decarbonisation," *European Energy Review*, December 12, 2011. http://www.europeanenergyrevieweu/site/pagina.php?id=3417.

75. Richard Marsh and Tom Miers, "Worth the Candle? The Economic Impact of Renewable Energy Policy in Scotland and the UK," Verso Economics, March 2011, http://www.versoeconomics.com/ verso-0311B.pdf.

76. Tait Trussell, "Wind Power Is Dying," August 28, 2011, http://frontpagemag.com/2011/08/28/wind-power-is-dying/.

77. A January 2007 settlement agreement, in which operators at Altamont agreed to a series of measures to reduce bird deaths by 50 percent, was found to have failed, with the same number of bird deaths as before the settlement. H. Sterling Burnett, "Altamont Pass Settlement Fails to Reduce Bird Kills," *Environment & Climate News*, March 2008.

78. Quoted in Katie Pavlich, "Oops: Greenies Killing Thousands of Protected Birds," August 16, 2011, http://townhall.com/tipsheet/ katiepavlich/2011/08/16/oops_greenies_killing_thousands_of_p rotected_birds_daily.

79. "A Bird-Brained Prosecution," unsigned, *The Wall Street Journal*, September 29, 2011, http://online.wsj.com/article/ SB10001424053111903791504576588642920063046.html?m od=ITP_opinion_2.

80. For example, the cost of building transmission lines for wind power in Texas is coming in 40 percent higher than original estimates – $6.8 billion rather than the $4.9 billion projected in 2008. This amounts to $800 per Texas household. See Kenneth Artz, "Texas Wind Power Lines Bust Budget, *Environment & Climate News*, November 2011, http://news.heartland.org/newspaper-article/2011/09/26/wind-power-lines-busting-budget-texas.

81. Steve Pociask and Joseph P. Fuhr Jr., "Progress Denied: A Study on the Potential Economic Impact of Permitting Challenges Facing Proposed Energy Projects," TeleNomic Research, LLC, March 10 2011, http://www.projectnoproject.com/wp-content/uploads/2011/03/PNP_EconomicStudy.pdf.

82. "Conneticut Renewable Portfolio Standard. Database of State Incentives for Renewables and Efficiency," U.S. Department of Energy. August 30, 2011, http://www.dsireusa.org/incentives/incentive.cfm?Incentive_Code=CT04R&re=1&ee=1.

83. New Mexico Renewable Portfolio Standard, Database of State Incentives for Renewables and Efficiency, U.S. Department of Energy. August 4, 2011, http://www.dsireusa.org/incentives/incentive.cfm?Incentive_Code=NM05R&re=1&ee=1.

84. California Renewable Portfolio Standard, Database of State Incentives for Renewables and Efficiency, U.S. Department of Energy, April 12, 2011.

85. Bonner R. Cohen, "Renewables to Jolt LA Electricity Rates," *Environment & Climate News*, May 2010. Cohen notes that even the global warming-supportive *Los Angeles Times* editorial board called the proposal "disconcerting."

86. Quoted in *Civil Defense Perspectives*, Physicians for Civil Defense, Tucson, Arizona, November 2010.

87. An auction held in June 2011 was a bust, the most unsuccessful of 12 that have been held since the program started in 2008. Ric Werme, "12th Quarterly RGGI Auction a Bust? It Sure Wasn't a Boom," http://WattsUpwiththat.com/2011/06/11.

88. Gina Morse-Cheeseman, "New Jersey Leaves the Regional Greenhouse Gas Initiative," TriplePundit, May 30, 2011. The remaining nine states in the program are Connecticut, Delaware, Maine, Maryland, Massachusetts, New Hampshire, New York, Rhode Island, and Vermont. A suit has been filed in New York seeking to force the state to withdraw, claiming participation involves an illegal tax imposed by the governor without approval of the state legislature. See Bonner R. Cohen, "Hard Times Hit Carbon-Trading Markets," *Environment & Climate News*, August 2011.

89. "Midwest Greenhouse Gas Reduction Accord," Pew Center on Global Climate Change, http://www.pewclimate.org/what_s_being_done/ in_the_states/mggra.

90. *The Energy Advocate*, March 2011. Quoted in *Civil Defense Perspectives*, Physicians for Civil Defense, Tucson, Arizona, May 2011.

91. *Massachusetts v. U.S. EPA*, 127 S. Ct. 1438, 1458 (2007).

92. *Ibid.*, at 1467.

93. *Ibid.*, at 1472.

94. Krystle Russin, "EPA Scientist Carlin Explains his Dissent on Endangerment Finding," *Environment & Climate News*, October 2009, http://news.heartland.org/newspaper-article/2009/10/01/epa-sci entist-carlin-explains-his-dissent-endangerment-finding.

95. Alexandra Liddy Bourne, "Input Sought on EPA Plan to Restrict CO2," *Environment & Climate News*, November 2008.

96. Ben Lieberman and Nicolas Loris, "Five Reasons the EPA Should Not Regulate CO2," April 25, 2009,http://www.speroforum.com/a/19046/ Five-reasons-the-EPA-should-not-regulate-CO2.

97. Goreham, *supra* note 5, p. 157.

98. *Ibid.*

99. Isaac and Isaac, *supra* note 2, pp. 45–46.

100. The superior record of nuclear power was a constant theme of Petr Beckmann's publication *Access to Energy*. See, for example, Petr Beckmann, "What's a Few More Widows?" *Access to Energy*, 1 March 1979 (Vol. 6, No. 7).

101. Isaac and Isaac, *supra* note 2, p. 66.

102. *Ibid.*, p. 76.

103. *Ibid.*, p. 7.

104. *Ibid.*

105. Quoted in Goreham, *supra* note 5, p. 250.

106. Isaac and Isaac, *supra* note 2, p. 69.

107. *Ibid.*, pp. 80–81.

108. Richard Stengel, "A Prince and His Princess Arrive," *Time Magazine World*, June 24, 2001, http://www.time.com/time/magazine/ article/0,9171,142818,00.html#ixzz1fHnJOPDY. Stengel writes: "Charles is attracted to certain strains of New Age thinking. He longs to combine pragmatism with compassion. He is an admirer of the 'small is beautiful' philosophy of the British economist E.F. Schumacher, and is a patron of the charity that Schumacher started to help Third World nations develop simple industrial and agricultural tools.

109. Isaac and Isaac, *supra* note 2, p. 68.

110. Quoted by Dixie Lee Ray, "The Media and the Economy," address to 1992 Progress Foundation International Economic Conference, Zurich, Switzerland.

111. See http://en.wikipedia.org/wiki/Pedicularis_furbishiae.

112. Isaac and Isaac, *supra* note 2, pp. 77–78.

113. Landes, *supra* note 1, p. 100.

114. Isaac and Isaac, *supra* note 2, p. 233.

115. *Ibid.*, pp. 233–34.

116. *Ibid.*, p. 234.

117. *Ibid.*, p. 66.

118. *Ibid.*, p. 225.

119. *Ibid.*, p. 225.

120. "Time Magazine Announces Approaching Ice Age," http://anotherviewonclimate.wordpress.com/2010/01/15/time-announces-approaching-ice-age/.

121. James M. Taylor, "Global Warming Alarmists Are in Denial," *Environment & Climate News*, July 2010.

122. Quoted in Goreham, *supra* note 5, p. 347.

123. *Ibid.*, p. 348.

124. Quoted in Bell, *supra* note 12, p. 206.

125. *Ibid.*

126. Stephen Moore, "How North Dakota Became Saudi Arabia: The Weekend Interview with Harold Hamm," *The Wall Street Journal*, October 1, 2011.

127. Landes, *supra* note 1, pp. 113–14.

128. Goreham, *supra* note 5, p. 2.

129. Obama's statement about coal was never published, but was revealed by a tape recording of the interview he gave to the *San Francisco Chronicle*. During the interview Obama promised to use the "huge sums" to be extracted from coal producers and other fossil fuel plants to generate billions of dollars "to invest" in solar, wind, and other alternative energy approaches. "Audio: Obama Tells San Francisco Chronicle He Will Bankrupt Coal Industry," P.J. Gladnick, November 2, 2008, http://newsbusters.org/blogs/p-j-gladnick/2008/11/02/ audio-obama-tells-sf-chronicle-he-will-bankrupt-coal-industry.

130. Eric Cantor, "Memo on Upcoming Jobs Agenda," August 29, 2011, http://majorityleader.gov/blog/2011/08/ memo-on-upcoming-jobs-agenda.html.

131. James M. Taylor, "New EPA Regulations Blamed as Power Plants Close, Jobs Disappear," *Environment & Climate News*, July 2011.

132. "Inside the EPA," unsigned, *The Wall Street Journal*, September 26, 2011, http://online.wsj.com/article/ SB10001424053111904194604576582814196136594.html.

133. In contrast to the 81 gigawatts we are likely to lose from the shutdown of coal plants, Brightsource, the company building Ivanpah, estimates it will provide 400 megawatts of energy. http://www.brightsourceenergy.com/images/uploads/ Brightsource_Ivanpah_Fast_Facts.pdf.

134. In January 2009 a conference on polar bears was held in Winnipeg. Canadian Environment Minister Jim Prentice received starkly different reports from scientists and the Inuit people who lived in the region. Alarmist scientists warned vanishing sea ice and over-hunting threatened the polar bear populations, while Inuit leaders spoke of "bear populations doubling over the last 50 years, proliferating to the point of becoming a pest in many northern communities." Goreham, *supra* note 5, pp. 125–6.

135. "Critics take aim at polar bear listing," *USA Today*, March 7, 2007, http://www.usatoday.com/weather/climate/globalwarming/2007-03-03-polar-bears_N.htm.

136. Bonner R. Cohen, "Administration Blocks Virginia's Off-Shore Drilling Plans," *Environment & Climate News*, April 2010.

137. Dan Springer, "Energy in America: EPA Rules Force Shell to Abandon Oil Drilling Plans," Fox News, April 25, 2011, http://www.foxnews.com/us/2011/04/25/energy-america-oil-drilling-denial/#ixzz1cabNxRpi.

138. "Exxon Tries Bear Wrestling," unsigned, *The Wall Street Journal*, September 2, 2011.

139. Lucian Pugliaresi, "The Lessons of the Shale Gas Revolution," *The Wall Street Journal*, September 30, 2011. Exxon seems to believe even Russia is a better bet despite the well-known hazards of doing business with Vladimir Putin. The company is committing billions to drilling in Russia's Arctic seas. See "Exxon Tries Bear Wrestling," *ibid*.

140. Russell Gold, "Exxon, U.S. Government Duel Over Huge Oil Find," *The Wall Street Journal*, August 18, 2011, http://online.wsj.com/article/SB10001424053111903596904576514762275032794.html.

141. Cohen, *supra* note 136.

142. John Podesta, "Natural Gas: A Bridge Fuel for the 21st Century," http://www.americanprogress.org/issues/2009/08/bridge_fuel.html.

143. Robert Bryce, "Five Rules about Climate Change," *The Wall Street Journal*, October 6, 2011, http://online.wsj.com/article/SB10001424052970203388804576612620828387968.html.

144. "Evaluation of Impacts to Underground Sources of Drinking Water by Hydraulic Fracturing of Coalbed Methane Reservoirs – Executive Summary," U.S. Environmental Protection Agency, June 2004, http://www.epa.gov/ogwdw/uic/pdfs/cbmstudy_attach_uic_exec_summ.pdf.

145. Ada Kulesza, "Natural Disaster: How Did the Gas Industry Get So Fracked Up?" *Philadelphia Weekly*, September 14, 2011.

146. Investigative journalists discovered methane-rich natural gas is so prevalent in the area that residents have been able to light their water on fire since at least the 1930s, long before hydraulic fracturing. If anything, natural gas extraction – through hydraulic fracturing or other methods – is likely to reduce the naturally occurring contamination of regional water. See James M. Taylor, "Hydraulic Fracturing (Fracking) of Natural Gas," *Research & Commentary*, The Heartland Institute, June 21, 2011, http://heartland.org/policy-documents/research-commentary-hydraulic-fracturing-fracking-natural-gas.

147. Kathleen Hartnett White, "The Fracas About Fracking," *National Review*, June 20, 2011.

148. *Ibid.*

149. Steve Milloy, "EPA to Issue 1-2 Year Moratorium on Fracking?" Canada Free Press, November 30, 2011, http://www.canadafreepress.com/index.php/article/42835.

150. Rich Trzupek, *Regulators Gone Wild* (New York, NY: Encounter Books, 2011), p. 118.

151. Deborah Solomon, "SEC Bears Down on Fracking," *The Wall Street Journal*, August 25, 2011, http://online.wsj.com/article/SB10001424053111904009304576528484179638702.html.

152. Matthew Brown, "Oil and gas leases put on hold in Montana, Dakotas," AgWeek.com, April 9, 2010, http://www.agweek.com/event/article/id/16107/.

153. Bonner R. Cohen, "New Utah Law Challenges Federal Lands Expansion," *Environment & Climate News*, May 2010.

154. "Protecting Wilderness Characteristics on Lands Managed by the Bureau of Land Management," Secretarial Order No. 3310, U.S. Department of the Interior, December 22, 2010, http://www.blm.gov/pgdata/etc/medialib/blm/wo/Communication s_Directorate/public_affairs/news_release_attachments.Par.26 564.File.dat/sec_order_3310.pdf.

155. "Salazar Outlines Broad Opportunities for Common Ground on Wilderness," U.S. Department of the Interior, June 1, 2011, http://www.blm.gov/wo/st/en/info/newsroom/ 2011/june/NR_06_01_2011.html.

156. Cohen, *supra* note 153.

157. Patrick Manning, "Saving the Dunes Sagebrush Lizard Could Endanger Oil Production, Lawmakers Say," Fox News, May 10, 2011, http://www.foxnews.com/politics/ 2011/05/10/saving-dunes-sagebrush-lizard-kill-oil-production/#i xzz1cbcpiYdB.

158. Jeff Mason, "Obama Steps Up Nuclear Investment," Reuters, February 16, 2010, http://www.reuters.com/article/ 2010/02/16/climate-nuclear-idUSN1622469320100216.

159. Sunlen Miller, "Obama Says Safe Nuclear Plants Are a Necessary Investment," ABC News, February 16, 2010, http://abcnews.go.com/blogs/politics/2010/02/obama-says-safe -nuclear-power-plants-are-a-necessary-investment/.

160. "Salazar's Priorities," unsigned, *The Wall Street Journal*, September 23, 2011, http://online.wsj.com/article/ SB10001424053111904060604576573000173005420.html.

161. "Obama's Nuclear Calculation Not Likely to Bear Fruit," unsigned, Spiegel Online, February 18, 2010, http://www.spiegel.de/international/world/0,1518,678774.00.ht ml.

162. Suzanne Goldenberg, "Obama Focuses on Green Economy in Speech Before Congress," *The Guardian* (UK), February 24, 2009, http://www.guardian.co.uk/world/2009/feb/25/barack-obama-green-economy-environment.

163. Ann West, "The Case Against the Use of Wind Farms in the UK," Farmers Weekly Interactive, February 1, 2007, http://www.fwi.co.uk/Articles/01/02/2007/101373/The-case-against-the-use-of-wind-farms-in-the-UK.htm.

164. See for example Rich Trzupek, "Solargate Spreads," September 30, 2011, http://frontpagemag.com/2011/09/30/solargate-spreads/. See also Holman Jenkins, "The Real Solyndra Scandal," *The Wall Street Journal*, September 29, 2011, http://online.wsj.com/article/SB10001424052970204422404576596583020868662.html.

165. Ryan Tracy, "Official Tied to Solyndra Loan Deal Is Departing," *The Wall Street Journal*, October 7, 2011, http://online.wsj.com/article/SB10001424052970203476804576615333630677742.html?mod=ITP_pageone_1.

166. Isaac and Isaac, *supra* note 2, p. 66.

167. "Desert Tortoise Holds Up Calif. Solar Power Plant," ABC News, July 26, 2011, http://abcnews.go.com/Technology/video/desert-tortoise-habitat-law-suit-holds-california-solar-power-plant-mojave-14161513.

168. Rael Jean Isaac, "Environmentalists vs. Renewable Energy," *Environment & Climate News*, August 2011. Where solar and wind projects should be built is a slippery issue. The Natural Resources Defense Council and National Audubon Society released a Google Earth map of the western United States showing areas they believed should be off-limits for renewable energy development. Three weeks later the NRDC issued a clarification – it did not mean to green-light the remaining areas.

169. Ryan Tracy, "Court Overturns Key Cape Wind Clearance," *The Wall Street Journal*, October 28, 2011, http://online.wsj.com/article/ SB10001424052970203687504577003921827695452.html.

170. Christopher Booker, "Wind Farms: The Monuments to Lunacy That Will Be Left Behind to Blot the Landscape," *The Telegraph* (UK), September 10, 2011.

171. Trzupek, *supra* note 150.

172. Paul Driessen, "Obama Administration, Environmental Lobby Responsible for Low Oil Reserves," *Environment & Climate News*, July 2011.

173. Goreham, *supra* note 5, p. 166.

174. *Ibid.*, p. 166.

175. Robinson, Robinson, and Soon, *supra* note 46.

176. *Ibid.*

177. "The Facts about Fracking," unsigned, *The Wall Street Journal*, June 25, 2011, http://online.wsj.com/article/ SB10001424052702303936704576398462932810874.html.

178. Steve Gelsi, "Chesapeake's Plan To Seed Natural-Gas Market Wins Praise Of Analysts," *The Wall Street Journal*, July 12, 2011, http://online.wsj.com/article/ BT-CO-20110712-712526.html.

179. Ben Lefebvre, "Gas-to-Liquid Site May Hit $10 Billion," *The Wall Street Journal*, September 14, 2011, http://online.wsj.com/article/ SB10001424053111904353504576568872584676488.html.

180. Clare Ansberry, "Left for Extinct, a Steel Plant Rises in Ohio," *The Wall Street Journal*, August 2, 2011, http://online.wsj.com/article/ SB10001424053111904233404576462562705511704.html.

181. *Ibid.*

182. Cal Dooley, "Shale Gas Is Helping Industry, Too," *The Wall Street Journal*, August 5, 2011, http://online.wsj.com/article/ SB10001424053111903454504576486390548600586.html.

183. Christopher Booker "The BBC Steadfastly Avoids the Facts About the Wind Farm Scam," *The Telegraph* (UK), August 20, 2011.

184. Max Colchester, "French Primary Reflects a Shift on Nuclear Power," *The Wall Street Journal*, October 14, 2011, http://online.wsj.com/article/SB10001424052970204774604576 628900180745680.html.

185. Christopher Booker, "The Lights May Go Out in Germany Even Sooner than in Britain," *The Telegraph* (UK), September 3, 2011.

186. Laura Gitschier and Alexander Neubacher, "German 'Energy Revolution' Depends on Nuclear Imports," *Der Spiegel*, September 15, 2011.

187. See, for example, Christopher Horner, "Leaked Document Shows Spain's 'Green' Policies Are An Economic Disaster," Global Warming Policy Foundation, May 29, 2010, http://www.thegwpf.org/international-news/974-leaked-docume nt-shows-spains-green-policies-are-an-economic-disaster.html.

188. Christopher Horner, "Leaked Doc Proves Spain's 'Green' Policies — the Basis for Obama's — an Economic Disaster (PJM Exclusive)," May 18, 2010, http://pjmedia.com/blog/spains-green-policies-an -economic-disaster/.

189. Ben Sills, "Spain Pricks Solar Power Bubble to Avoid Greece's Fate," April 30, 2010, http://www.bloomberg.com/news/2010-04-29/ spain-pricks-solar-bubble-and-loses-investors-to-avoid-greek-st yle-crisis.html.

190. Charles River Associates, *Indian Point Energy Center Retirement Analysis*, August 2, 2011, http://www.crai.com/uploadedFiles/Publications/Indian_Point_E nergy_Center_Retirement_Analysis.pdf; and New York Building Congress, *Electricity OUTLOOK: Powering New York City through 2030*, October 2011, http://www.buildingcongress.com/research/electricity/2011-05.h tml.

191. "The Midwest Wind Surtax," unsigned, *The Wall Street Journal*, December 30, 2010, http://online.wsj.com/article/ SB10001424052970204527804576043893513811886.html.

192. "Inside the EPA," unsigned, *The Wall Street Journal*, September 26, 2011, http://online.wsj.com/article/ SB10001424053111904194604576582814196136594.html.

193. "Government vs. EPA," unsigned, *The Wall Street Journal*, October 12, 2011, http://online.wsj.com/article/ SB10001424052970203633104576625091826666516.html.

194. Bonner R. Cohen "Gulf Ecology Recovering from Oil Spill," *Environment & Climate News*, September 2010.

195. Thomas L. Friedman, "Is it Weird Enough Yet?" *The New York Times*, September 14, 2011, http://www.nytimes.com/2011/09/14/ opinion/friedman-is-it-weird-enough-yet.html.

196. Jeff Jacoby, "Climate Skeptics Don't Deny Science," *The Boston Globe*, September 24, 2011.

197. Bell, *supra* note 12, p. 15.

198. "Climate sceptism 'on the rise,' BBC poll shows," February 7, 2010, http://news.bbc.co.uk/2/hi/8500443.stm.

199. "Public's Priorities for 2010: Economy, Jobs, Terrorism," Pew Research Center for the People & the Press, January 25, 2010, http://www.people-press.org/2010/01/25/ publics-priorities-for-2010-economy-jobs-terrorism/.

200. "Notable and Quotable," *The Wall Street Journal*, August 23, 2011, http://online.wsj.com/article/ SB10001424053111903461304576524621622255138.html.

201. "Global Warming Cools Off as Top Concern," Nielsen Business Wire, August 28, 2011, http://www.businesswire.com/ news/home/20110828005020/en/Global-Warming-Cools-Top-C oncern.

202. *Climate Change 2007: The Physical Science Basis. Contribution of Working Group I to the Fourth Assessment Report of the Intergovernmental Panel on Climate Change* (Cambridge, UK: Cambridge University Press, 2007); *Climate Change Reconsidered*, *supra* note 30.

203. Fraser Nelson, "The Osborne Doctrine," *The Spectator*, October 7, 2011. The article reports Osborne was in a minority, but not a small minority, in departing from the party's green orthodoxy.

204. "The Post-Global Warming World," unsigned, *The Wall Street Journal*, October 25, 2011, http://online.wsj.com/article/ SB10001424052970204618704576640730949448812.html.

205. The climate talks in Cancun in 2010 produced no agreement, and those at Durban on November 28–December 9, 2011 were expected to fare no better, with the United States, Russia, and Japan having all said in advance they will not agree to a new binding pact. Unexpectedly, a pact was cobbled together, signed by 200 countries, including the U.S., Russia and Japan, which kicked the can down the road to 2015, when delegates agreed to draft a new global emissions treaty to take effect in 2020. Even then China and India refused to contemplate accepting a "legal instrument" to police emissions cuts so instead the phrase "legal force" was used, whatever that means. (Patrick McGroarty, "China, India, U.S. Take Steps Toward Emissions Deal," *The Wall Street Journal*, December 12, 2011)

206. "EU Weighs Pullback on Cutting Emissions," unsigned, *The Wall Street Journal*, October 19, 2011, http://online.wsj.com/article/ SB10001424052970204346104576638634143967012.html.

207. This is not a foregone conclusion. Even within the European Commission there are those committed to lowering emissions regardless of economic consequences. A climate change department within the commission is likely to resist any attempt to water down the European Union's green credentials and has been in conflict with the energy department before. See Alexander Torello, "Europe Reconsidering Its Unilateral Climate Policy," *The Wall Street Journal* (Europe), October 18, 2011.

208. Quoted by Vaclav Klaus, "Human Freedom, Not Climate, Is at Risk," *Environment & Climate News*, September 2007.

209. Katie Glueck, "Bloomberg Gives Sierra Club $50 Million to Fight Coal Plants," *The Wall Street Journal*, July 22, 2011, http://blogs.wsj.com/washwire/2011/07/21/bloomberg-gives-sierra-club-50-million-to-fight-coal-plants/.

210. Bell, *supra* note 12, p. 102.

211. Mark Steyn, *After America: Get Ready for Armageddon* (Washington, DC: Regnery, 2011), p. 52.

212. Kate Galbraith, "An Environmental Brain Drain to DC," *The New York Times*, April 7, 2009. See also "NRDC Mafia: Finding Homes on Hill, in EPA," Greenwire, March 6, 2009.

213. Quoted by Steyn, *supra* note 211, p. 325.

214. Trzupek, *supra* note 150, p. 136.

215. *Ibid.*, pp. 136-37.

216. George Russell, "EPA Ponders Expanded Regulatory Power in Name of 'Sustainable Development.'" Russell notes EPA head Sheila Jackson called this study "the next phase of

environmental protection" and said it was "fundamental to the future of the EPA." http://www.foxnews.com/politics/2011/12/19/epa-ponders-expanded-regulatory-power-in-name-sustainable-development/print#ixzz1h7TChyr9.

217. *Sustainability and the U.S. EPA*, National Academy of Sciences, August 2011, p. 3. http://sites.nationalacademies.org/PGA/sustainability/EPA/index.htm.

218. Glenn M. Ricketts, "The Roots of Sustainability," *Academic Questions*, Spring 2010, p. 44.

219. *Sustainability and the U.S. EPA*, supra note 217, p. 8.

220. *Ibid.*, pp. 5, 24, 26, 28.

221. Ricketts, *supra* note 218, p. 33. This is biologist and anti-nuclear activist Barry Commoner's first law of economy and requires, Ricketts writes, "an all-encompassing preventative regime in which present day consumption has to be judged, moment by moment, against an imagined and imaginary future."

222. Quoted by Steyn, *supra* note 211, p. 140.

223. Mary Anastasia O'Grady, "Canada's Oil Sands Are a Jobs Gusher," *The Wall Street Journal*, September 12, 2011.

224. Deborah Solomon, "U.S. Delays Pipeline Decision," *The Wall Street Journal*, November 11, 2011, http://online.wsj.com/article/SB10001424052970204358004577030093417692560.html.

225. *Ibid.* O'Sullivan also feared the delay – and proposed rerouting of the pipeline in Nebraska, something the State Department had considered earlier and determined was impracticable – would prove fatal to the project.

226. "Relaxation of Obama's Anti-Energy Policies Could Create 1.4 Million New Jobs," Oilprice.com, September 14, 2011, http://oilprice.com/Energy/Energy-General/Relaxation-of-Obamas-Anti-Energy-Policies-Could-Create-1.4-Million-New-Jobs.html.

227. Cheryl K. Chumley, "EPA Asserts More Control Over States," *Environment & Climate News*, July 2011.

228. Metin Celebi, "Potential Coal Plant Retirements and Retrofits Under Emerging Environmental Regulations," The Brattle Group, presentation to MREA, St Cloud, Minnesota, August 10, 2010, www.thebrattlegroup.org/_documents/UploadLibrary/Upload981.pdf.

229. Bonner R. Cohen, *supra* note 153.

230. Ibid.